International Inventions

LONDON, 1885.

GUIDE

TO THE

LOAN COLLECTION

AND LIST OF

MUSICAL INSTRUMENTS, MANUSCRIPTS, BOOKS, PAINTINGS, AND ENGRAVINGS,

EXHIBITED IN THE

GALLERY AND LOWER ROOMS OF THE ALBERT HALL.

PRINTED AND PUBLISHED FOR THE

𝕰𝔵𝔢𝔠𝔲𝔱𝔦𝔟𝔢 𝕮𝔬𝔲𝔫𝔠𝔦𝔩 𝔬𝔣 𝔱𝔥𝔢 𝕴𝔫𝔱𝔢𝔯𝔫𝔞𝔱𝔦𝔬𝔫𝔞𝔩 𝕴𝔫𝔟𝔢𝔫𝔱𝔦𝔬𝔫𝔰 𝕰𝔵𝔥𝔦𝔟𝔦𝔱𝔦𝔬𝔫,
𝔞𝔫𝔡 𝔣𝔬𝔯 𝔱𝔥𝔢 𝕮𝔬𝔲𝔫𝔠𝔦𝔩 𝔬𝔣 𝔱𝔥𝔢 𝕾𝔬𝔠𝔦𝔢𝔱𝔶 𝔬𝔣 𝕬𝔯𝔱𝔰,

BY

WILLIAM CLOWES AND SONS, LIMITED,

INTERNATIONAL INVENTIONS EXHIBITION,

AND 13, CHARING CROSS, S.W.

1885.

PREFACE.

THE intention of the Loan Collection of Musical Instruments, Manuscripts, Books, Paintings, and Engravings, exhibited in the Gallery and lower rooms of the Royal Albert Hall, is to show the historic development of the Art of Music, by the comparative kinds and structure of different instruments; the means employed to note and record musical sounds and expression; the portraits and autographs of eminent musicians, and the ideas that have been excited in a sister art by musical suggestion. Subordinate to the musical interest, but not less important for an historical survey of culture, is the decoration employed to make musical instruments a source of pleasure to the eye, and intimately connected with this refined adornment is the feeling for graceful lines which is shown in fine violins, or the fancy and colour which make every page of an old Antiphoner or Gradual a pleasure to behold. Perhaps in the famous Cremona violins the combination of satisfaction to the senses is the most complete. Inventive progress may be traced in the three hundred years during which spinets and harpsichords were paramount as keyed stringed instruments, but to give way ultimately to pianofortes, the culmination of which may be seen in those shewn in the Gallery which, made in the last few years, have been chosen for the genius of great living painters—of Mr. Alma Tadema and of Mr. Burne Jones — to make beautiful.

The initiation of this important Exhibition, by far the most complete ever brought together in any country, is due to H.R.H. the Prince of Wales, the President of the International Inventions Exhibition. It happily occurred to His Royal Highness, in establishing a Division for Music in the present Exhibition, to follow the precedent set forth in the London International Exhibition held at South Kensington in 1872, by supplementing it with a Loan Collection. The success of the small but comprehensive Loan Exhibition of that year which took place in the South Kensington Museum has not been forgotten. It was thought by some persons that a similar collection could hardly again be formed. The public spirit of amateurs in this country and elsewhere has replied effectively to this doubt by the present much larger and more important one. Her Majesty the Queen has most liberally contributed to it from Windsor Castle, Buckingham and St. James's Palaces. The friendly and liberal support of the Belgian Government has permitted the transference of an important section of the Museum of the Brussels Conservatoire to the Royal Albert Hall, and by the personal co-operation of the Director of the Museum, M. Victor Mahillon, musical instruments of the past have been worthily heard in Historical Musical Performances that have already taken place in the Music Room of the Exhibition. Another idea has found its fulfilment through the taste and public spirit of Mr. George Donaldson. This has been the erection of Historic Rooms, which, with the fittings and furniture of the period represented, combine the presence of those musical instruments which were then in domestic use. For instance, the Early Eighteenth Century Room contains the spinet, the viola da gamba, and the viola d'amore. The Tudor Room, the spinet that was Queen Elizabeth's; and the Louis Seize Room, Lord Powercourt's beautifully-painted harpsichord, the former possession of which is attributed to Marie Antoinette. It will be found most convenient to visitors to begin the examination of the Loan Collection from these rooms. By doing so, and immediately following Mr. Donaldson's own collection of lutes, mandolines and guitars, a remarkable. collection of the violin family may be seen in due order, comprising an adequate show of the much-neglected English. School, leading up to the finest examples of the Italian. Schools, the masterpieces of Brescia and Cremona—of Stradiuarius and Guarnerius del Gesu. The pianofortes already mentioned, with one adorned by paintings transferred from a harpsichord that belonged to Anne of Austria, and is now lent by Her Majesty the Queen, have important positions. The fine Brussels Conservatoire Collection, includes rare specimens of the Positive organ and Regals, the Patavini spinet, the only existing complete set of cromornes, with other curious wind instruments, and stringed tromba marina. The lute, or rather orpheoreon from Helmingham, believed to have been Queen Elizabeth's, the Scottish Highland "Queen Mary," and "Lamont" harps, the harpsichord that was Maria Theresa's, and instruments no less interesting, but to name which would occupy space not to be spared in what is intended to be no more than a brief introduction, will be found worthy of study. We must not, however, omit to mention the guitar and the cetera made by Stradiuarius, the last-named instrument a marvel of fine art, nor the upright spinet from the Correr Collection at Venice, which obviously of the last years of the fifteenth century is the oldest instrument of the clavier family yet recorded. Passing by the pictures and engravings which are of great interest, especially in portraits, we have to point out the arrangement of manuscripts and books in order of time which, beginning with the rare mediæval contributions from the Monastery of St. Gall, form a complete history of Modern Music. Lord Spencer's priceless Mentz Psalter, one of the first printed books, should not be passed by unnoticed. Among the autographs are to be seen MSS. of Handel selected from Buckingham Palace, his Will, and also one of the Ruffles that he wore. In conjunction with the portraits of this great composer and the Vauxhall statue by Roubiliac, the Bi-centenary of his birth is here commemorated by a group of objects in themselves sufficient to form a special Handel exhibition. Adjacent to the sketch-books of Beethoven there is a document described as his Will, which is sadly indicative of that composer's peculiar emotional temperament, and the mask of Beethoven's face, taken four years before his death, that arrests attention by its strong life-like expression. In the lower rooms, near the Conservatory, will be found numerous claviohords, harpsichords, and spinets, the very complete Indian Collection originally formed by the Rajah Sourindro Mohun Tagore, and a fine collection of instruments from Java that belonged to the late Sir Stamford Raffles. It will be interesting to compare with these, although not in the Loan Collection, the beautiful instruments of similar kinds shown in the East Central Gallery, under the tent near the Music Room of the Exhibition, sent by the King of Siam.

A. J. HIPKINS.

CONTENTS.

Note.—The Division Numbers given in the Catalogue correspond to those painted in large figures in each division of the Gallery of the Royal Albert Hall.

The objects in the centre (or numbered) cases in each division are first enumerated, then those in the Wall Cases, and lastly the pictures, engravings, &c., on the walls and pillars of the Gallery.

In the additional rooms the objects in the centre have first been catalogued, and afterwards those on or near the walls, from left to right, on entering the doorways from the Conservatory Staircase.

CATALOGUE.

DIVISION 1.

Case I.
DONALDSON, Mr. GEORGE.—*Mandoline*, Milanese, c. 1700.
—— *Viola d'Amore*, by J. N. Eberle. Prague.
—— *Kit*, English. 18th century.
—— *Guitar*, Spanish. Late 16th century.
—— *Pochette*, by Matthias Albano. Tyrol, 1675.
—— *Viola d'Amore*, by J. M. Eberle. Prague.
—— *Mandoline*, Spanish. 1778.
—— *Archlute*, ivory, by Giovanni Krebar. Padua, 1629.
—— *Mandoline*, Neapolitan, by Domenico Vinaccia. 1730.
—— *Guitar*, Italian. 16th century. Tortoise-shell, with fleur-de-lys pegs. Said to have been Rizzio's.
—— *Mandoline*, Spanish, by Antonio Prada. 1778.
—— *Guitar*, Italian. 16th century.
—— *Pochette*, Italian. 1675.
—— *Giterna*, by Joachim Tielke. Hamburg, 1676.
—— *Sordino*, Cremonese. Probably by Amati.
—— *Mandoline*, Milanese. 1775.
—— *Violin*, Italian, carved back.

Case II.
TADEMA, Mr. L. ALMA, R.A.—*Grand Piano and Seat*, oak with inlays of ivory, tortoise-shell and mother-of-pearl, by John Broadwood & Sons. 1878. Designed by Mr. G. E. Fox. Inscribed with autographs of musicians; the silver panel of Orpheus, by Amendola.

Wall Case.
DONALDSON, Mr. GEORGE.—*Lute*, probably Spanish. About 1640.
—— *Violin*, carved head, with guitar screws and wire strings, French. 19th century.
—— *Lyre Guitar*, satin-wood, inlaid. Signed Roudehofr.
—— *Viola*, by A. & H. Amati. 1590.
—— *Mute Violin*, quaint form, English. About 1820.

B

DONALDSON, Mr. GEORGE.—*Violin*, oblong.

—— *Viol*, Italian. Probably 16th century.

—— *Kit*, in the form of a fish.

—— *Flûte à bec*, ivory, by Villars, French. About 1780.

—— *Viola d'Amore*, German. About 1700.

—— *Mute Violin.*

—— *Gigelira*, made of iron-wood, 2 octaves.

—— *Mandoline*, Milanese.

—— *Lute*, by Tieffenbrucker. Padua, 1507.

—— *Viola da Gamba*, English. About 1700.

—— *Guitar Case*, red leather, with the arms of the Dauphin and the cipher and crown of Louis XVI.

—— *Violin Case*, carved oak. Period of Louis XV.

—— *Viola da Gamba*, by Barak Norman.

—— *Bust* in wax, of Paganini.

—— *Case for Violin*, French. 18th century.

—— *Flute*, ivory, by James Wood, English. About 1820.

—— *Lute.*

—— *Guitar.*

—— *Viola da Gamba*, 1710, by Jeremias Wurfel.

—— *Cither*, English or German. 18th century.

—— *Violin Bow*, by Dodd. English.

—— *Guitar*, Spanish, belonged to Louis XVI.

Over Wall Case.

DONALDSON, Mr. GEORGE.—*Vielle* or *Hurdy Gurdy*, French. 17th century.

—— *Guitar Case.*

—— *Cither.*

—— *Serpent.*

—— *Case.*

—— *Case.*

—— *Dital Harp.*

—— *Harp*, French.

———

TADEMA, Mrs. ALMA.—*Pianino*, by JOHN Broadwood & Sons, with Paintings, by L. Alma Tadema, R.A.

BROADWOOD, Messrs. John, & SONS. — *Square Piano*, by Johannes Zumpe. 1766, London. The oldest square piano known to exist, 18 keys in the octave.

Screen A.

HIPKINS, Mr. JOHN.—Two Frames, containing Woodcuts of Pianofortes, etc. Engraved by the Lender, for the Encyclopædia Britannica.

SOUTH KENSINGTON MUSEUM.—Twelve Frames of Photographs of Musical Instruments.

FORT, Mr. C. H. K.—Wood Engraving, showing the East Front of the Organ in Salisbury Cathedral. 1710.
—— Wood Engraving of the Organ in Weingarten Abbey.

HILL, Mr. A. G.—Drawing of an Organ Case. Designed by the Lender.

PICTURES, &C.

OXFORD, UNIVERSITY OF.—1. Portrait of Philip Hayes.

BROWN, Mr. J. J.—2. "The Violin Player," by Zimmermann.

STREET, Mr. J. E.—3. Portrait of Dr. Arne.

COLNAGHI, Messrs.—4. Portrait of Signor Scalzi, circa 1738.

RENDALL, Mr. JNO.—5. Portrait of Dr. Boyce, by Sir Joshua Reynolds.

BETTLE, Mr. P.—6. St. Cecilia.

SPENCER, Earl.—7. "Masked Ball," by P. Code.

HUISH, Mr. MARCUS B.—8. A Conversation Piece, by Dirk Hals, 1614.

OXFORD, UNIVERSITY OF.—9. Portrait of William Hayes.

WOOD, Mr. WM.—10. "The Music Lesson."

BROWN, Mr. J. J—11. "The Guitar Player," by Lampheimer.

SELLE, Mr. W. C., Mus. Doc.—12. Violin and MS. Music, by Collier. 1698.

.—13. Man playing Violoncello.

HIPKINS, Miss EDITH.—14. "The Pianette," by the Lender.

.—15. Photographs of Paganini's Violin. (Original in the Museum at Genoa).

.—16. Viola da Gamba, by Joachim Tielke. (Original in Bavarian National Museum at Munich).

BROADWOOD, JOHN, & SONS, Messrs.—17. A Plan, Elevation, and View of a Grand Pianoforte made for the Prime Minister of Spain in 1796, designed by Sheraton.

OXFORD, UNIVERSITY OF.—18. Portrait.

HIPKINS, Miss EDITH.—19. " An English Harpsichord," by the Lender. 1883.

FULLEYLOVE, Mr. JNO.—20. " A 17th Century Virginal," from Lord De Tabley's Virginal, made by Phillip Jones, 1671.

COX, Mr. CORNELIUS.—21. Three Wedgwood Plaques— Apollo, Erato, and Terpsichore (*circa* 1780).

DIVISION 2.

THE MUSEO CIVICO, TURIN.—*Harpsichord*, lacquer case, by A. Ruckers, of Antwerp, 1636. Restored by Pascal Taskin, of Paris, 1782.

PICTURES, &C.

DUNCAN, Mr. J. CUTHBERTSON. — 22. Portrait of Nicolo Paganini.

CHAPPELL & Co., Messrs.—23. Portrait of J. B. Cramer, by Marlow.

BETTLE, Mr. P.—24. Portrait of Dupont, attributed to Gainsborough.

HORSLEY, Mrs.—25. Portrait of Peter von Winter, by W. Owen, R.A.

ASPA, ROSARIO.—26. Portrait of Robert Lindley, Violin-cellist, by Rosenberg.

JACKSON, Rev. J. C., M.A., F.R.A.S.—27. "Merry Makers on All Hallow's E'en," by M. Narveu.

SPENCER, Earl.—28. "Spanish Bagpiper," by Velasquez.

BUTLER, Mr. C—29. Panel of Triptych, "Madonna and Angels," Umbrian School, 14th Century.

SPENCER, Earl.—30. "Head of a Harper," by Sir Peter Lely.

JACKSON, Rev. J. C., M.A., F.R.A.S—31. "All is Vanity," by D. Teniers.

BUTLER, Mr. C.—32. "Madonna and Angels." Sienese School, 14th Century.
—— 33. "Madonna and Angels," by Jacopo da Casentini, 14th Century.

—34. "Board of Italian Harpsichord," by G. A. Licinio (Il Pordenone), 1484–1540.

YARBOROUGH, Earl of.—35. "Cupid Playing a Lute," by Titian.

HOLFORD, Mr. R. S.—36. "The Virgin and Child," by Garofolo.

MUSICIANS, ROYAL SOCIETY OF.—37. Portrait of Corelli
      „   „   „   38. Portrait of Geminiani.

DIVISION 3.

THE ENGLISH MAKERS.

Case III.

HILL, Messrs. W. E., & SONS.—*Violin*, English, by Bernard Simon Fendt, of London. Date about 1840.
—— *Violin*, English, by Jacob Fendt, of London. Date about 1840.
—— ,, ,, by Bernard Fendt, of London. Date about 1800.

WITHERS, Mr. G.—*Violin*, English, by Bernard Simon Fendt, of London. 1840. Amati copy.

HILL, Messrs. W. E., & SONS.—*Violin*, English, by John and Arthur Betts, of London. Date 1851. A reproduction of the "Betts" Stradiuarius.
—— *Violin*, English, made by Peter Wamsley, "at the Harp and Hautboy in Pickadilly." Date about 1740.
—— ,, ,, by Jacob Ford, of London. Date about 1790.
—— ,, ,, by Richard Duke, of London. Date about 1770.
—— *Kit*, English, by Betts. Date about 1780.
—— ,, ,, by Tobin. Date about 1800.
—— ,, probably Old German.

CROMPTON, Mr. W.—*Violin*, English, by Richard Duke, of London. Date about 1770.

ROWLAND, Mr.—*Violin*, English, by Barak Norman at the "Bass Viol" in St. Paul's Churchyard, London. Fecit 1719.

OAKLEY, Sir HERBERT.—*Violin*, ancient, without sides.

WILMOTT, Miss E. A.—*Pochette and Bow.*
—— *Kit.*
—— *Pochette.*
—— *Pochette.*
—— *Crwth.* This and another in Case IV. are rare specimens of this old Welsh instrument.

Case IV.

HILL, Messrs. W. E., & SONS.—*Violin*, English, by Thomas Kennedy, of Oxford Street, London. Date about 1830.

—— *Violin*, English, by Joseph Hill & Sons, makers, at the Harp and Flute in the Haymarket. Date about 1770.

—— „ „ by Lockey Hill, London. Date about 1720.

—— *Viola*, English—Made and sold by Joseph Hill, "at ye Violin, in Angel Court, Westminster." Date about 1750.

—— *Violin*, English, by Lockey Hill, London. Date about 1810.

—— „ „ by Nathaniel Cross, of London. Date about 1720.

—— „ „ by John Betts, of London. Date about 1780.

CRESPIN, Mr. C. H.—*Viola*, English, by Benjamin Banks, of Salisbury. Date 1780.

COUCHMAN, Mr. — *Violin*, English, by Johann Nicolaus Lentz, London, Fecit, near the Church, Chelsea. Date 1807.

LARPENT, Miss BEATRICE DE HOEHEPIED.—*Violin*, English, by John Betts, London. 1788.

OLDAKER, Mr. T.—*Violin*, English, by John Lott, of London. A good imitation of a Joseph Guarnerius.

WITHERS, Mr. G.—*Violin*, English, by John Comins. Date 1801. Pupil of Forster.

.—*Cither*.

.—*Cruth*.

Case V.

HILL, Messrs. W. E., & SONS.—*Violin*, by Vincenzo Panormo, made in Palermo, in 1766.

—— *Violin*, English, by Vincenzo Panormo, made in London. Date about 1770.

—— „ „ by Benjamin Banks, of Salisbury. Date about 1770.

—— „ „ made by John Barrett, "at ye Harp and Crown, in Pickadilly," London. Date about 1731.

—— „ „ by Daniel Parker, of London. About 1714.

HILL, Messrs. W. E. & SONS.—*Violin*, English, by Richard Tobin, of London. About 1800.

BAKER, Mr. T.—*Violin*, English, by Daniel Parker, of London. About 1715.

HILL, Messrs. W. E. & SONS.—*Violin*, English, by Jacob Rayman, "at ye Belle Yarde in Southwarke." Date about 1650.
—— *Violin*, English, by Richard Tobin, of London. Date about 1800.
—— „ „ by Jacob Rayman, "at ye Belle Yarde in Southwarke," London. Date about 1650.
—— „ „ by Thomas Urquhart, of London. Date 1666.

GREENWOOD, Dr.—*Violin*, English, by Edward Pamphilion, of London. Date about 1680.

OTTLEY, Mrs. EDWARD.—*Violin*, English, by Edward Pamphilion, of London. Date about 1680.

WALKER, Mr.—*Violin*, English, by Christopher Wise, in Vine Court, Bishopgate Without, London. 1650.

CRUISE, Dr. FRANCIS R.—*Violin*, Irish, by Perry, of Dublin. Date about 1800.

ARKWRIGHT, Mr. G. H.—*Viola*, English, by William Forster. Date 1788.

THE BRESCIAN SCHOOL.

Case VI.

BARRETT, Mr. W. L.—*Viola*, by Giovanni Paolo Maggini, of Brescia. 17th century.

SANDYS, Lt.-Col. T. MYLES.—*Viola*, Italian. Date about 1500. By Peregrino Zanetto, of Brescia.

One of the earliest known makers of the Brescian School. This specimen presents considerable interest as being one of the earliest known instruments of the violin family as distinct from the old viola.

CROMPTON, Mr. W.—*Viola*, Italian, by Gaspar di Salo of Brescia. Date about 1580.

CROALL, Mr. W. *Violin*, Italian, by Maggini of Brescia. Date about 1600.

MATTHEW, Mr. J. E.—*Viola*, Italian, by Giovanni Paolo, of Brescia. 1610,

SYMES, Mr. H. W.—Two *Violas*, Italian, by Gaspar di Salo, of Brescia. Date about 1580.

Two remarkable specimens from the Adam Collection. Referred to by Mr. G. Hart, in his work on the Violin, and in Groves' Dictionary of Music and Musicians.

CRESPIN, Mr. C. H.—*Viola*, Italian, 1640, by Giovanni Paolo Maggini. The back inlaid.

DUNCAN, Mr. G. CUTHBERTSON.—*Viola*, Italian, from the Paganini collection.

AMHERST, Mr. W. A. TYSSEN, M.P.—*Violin*, Italian, by Gaspar di Salo of Brescia. Date about 1580.

THE AMATI SCHOOL.

Case VII.

HILL, Messrs. W. E. & SONS.—*Violin*, by Joannes Baptista Ruggerius, of Cremona. Date about 1690.

KNOOP, Mr. JOHN.—*Violin*, Italian, by Nicolaus Amatus, of Cremona. Date 1645.

Known as "The Alard," having belonged to the player of that name. It is the one referred to by Fétis in his work on stringed instruments.

STAMP, Mr. W.—*Violin*, Italian, by Nicolaus Amatus, of Cremona. Date 1678. Formerly the property of Dr. Camidge, of York, and of the Rev. Wm. Blow.

HILL, Messrs. W. E., & SONS.—Collection of Old Pegs, Bridges, Tailpieces, Finger-boards, &c., used by Italian, French, German, and English makers.

GULL, Mr. W. C.—*Violin*, Italian, by Joannes Baptista Ruggerius, of Cremona. 1706.

ORCHAR, Mr. JAS. G.—*Violin*, Italian. Antonius and Hieronymus Amati, of Cremona.

MUIRHEAD, Mr. H. J.—*Violin*, Italian, by Francesco Ruggerius, of Cremona. Date about 1690.

SANDEMAN, Mr. E. A.—*Violin*, Italian, by Joannes Baptista Ruggerius, of Cremona. Date about 1700.

PETHERICK, Mr. HORACE.—*Violin*, Italian, small size, by Antonius and Hieronymus Amati. Date 1618.

Wall Case.

SELLE, Dr.—*Violin*, Modern English, eccentric shape, by Baker, of Bristol.

ENGELBACH, Mrs. A. A.—*Violoncello*, English. About 1800. By T. Dodd.

An English maker who claimed to have possessed the receipt for preparing the Cremona varnish.

VAN DER WEYER, Miss.—*Violin*, modern French, imitation of an old fiddle.

COOPER, Mr. W. WHITE.—*Violoncello*, English, by William Forster. Us·d by George IV. when Prince Regent.

KING, Mr. JAMES.—*Violin*, old German. Date about 1750.

ASHBURNHAM, Earl of.—*Violin*, Old English, double purfled.

BUTLER, Mr. FRANK H.—*Viola*, labelled Laurentius Storioni. Date 1790.

CHATTOCK, Mr. R. J.—*Violoncello*, English, by Jacob Rayman, "dwelling in Blackburn Street, Long Southwark." Date about 1640.

VENABLES, Messrs. C. & Co.—*Violin*, English. Date about 1840.

WITHERS, Mr. G.—*Violin*, English, by G. Taylor. 1798.

HILL, Messrs. W. E., & SONS.—*Violoncello*, English, by Georgius Panormo, Felius Vincento Panormo, Londinensis, fecit A.D. 1836. Made for the late Earl of Liverpool.

ASHBURNHAM, Earl of.—*Violin*, Italian, back and ribs by Antonius Stradiuarius.

ALLEN, Mr. E. H.—*Spoon Fiddle*, Modern, cut out of solid pear-wood, with deal sounding-board.

WITHERS, Mr. G.—*Violin*, by Roysseaux. Aberdeen.

JACKSON, Mr. J.—*Violin*, Delft. 18th century.

PEINIGER, Herr.—Miniature Violin and Bows.

—— *Violin*.

—— „

—— „

—— „

—— *Violoncello*.

MOUGENOT, Mons.—*Violin,* copy of a Stradiuarius.
—— *Violin,* copy of a Maggini.

KIRKMAN & SON, Messrs.—*Double Harpsichord,* by Josephus
Kirkman. 1798. Venetiau Swell. London.

PICTURES, ETC.

DAVIS, Mr. J. HUNTER.—No. 39. Engraving by G. S.
Facius, after W. Owen, R.A. Portrait of Mr. J. P.
Salomon.

JACKSON, Mr. R.—No. 40. Engraving by J. L. Roullet, after
P. Migrard. Portrait of Jean Baptiste Lully.

ABERDEEN, Earl of.—No. 41. "The Singing Skull," by
Salvator Rosa.

HIPKINS, Mr. JOHN.—No. 42. Engravings of The Roses
(Trade Marks) of the Ruckers Family, by the Lender.
From Grove's Dictionary.

MUSICIANS, ROYAL SOCIETY OF.—No. 43. Portrait of
Haydn, the gift of Dr. Selle.

DIVISION 4.

THE AMATI SCHOOL.

Case VIII.

HOZIER, Lt.-Col.—*Violin*, Italian, by Antonius and Hieronymus Amati, of Cremona. Date 1608.

HILL, Messrs. W. E., & SONS.—*Violin*, large size, Italian, by Antonius and Hieronymus Amati, of Cremona. Date 1628.

ALLEN, Mr. E. HERON.—*Violin*, Early Italian, said to have been made by Andreas Amatus for Charles IX. of France. Painted with coat-of-arms and motto, " Quo unico propugnaculo."

ELPHINSTONE, Col. Sir HOWARD.—*Violin*, Italian, by Giofreda Cappa, pupil of Amati. Date about 1670.

FELLOWES, Mr. EDMUND HORACE. —*Violin*, Italian, by Nicolaus Amatus, of Cremona. Date 1679.

Formerly the property of the old glee writer, Stevens, who has scratched his name on the back and dated it Charterhouse, 1796.

BARRETT, Mr. W. LEWIS.—*Viola*, in its original large size, Italian, by Antonius and Hieronymus Amati, of Cremona. Date 1620.

PERKIN, Mr. T. D.—*Viola*, Italian, by Antonius and Hieronymus Amati, of Cremona. Date 1610.

H.M. THE QUEEN.—*Viola*, Italian, by Antonius and Hieronymus Amati, of Cremona. Painting on back of St. John the Baptist.

GIBSON, Mr. A.—*Viola*, Italian, by Hieronymus Amati, of Cremona. Date 1619. Formerly the property of the Earl of Aylesford.

SMITH, Rev. H. C.—*Violin*, labelled Nicolaus Amatus, of Cremona. Date 1673.

PIATTI, Signor.—*Violin*, Italian, by Hieronymus Amatus Filius Nicolai. Cremona. Date 1710.

SANDYS, Lieut.-Col. T. MYLES—*Viola*, Italian, by Antonius and Hieronymus Amati, of Cremona. Date 1616.

Painting of the Crucifixion on back and the Royal Arms of France. On the side the motto " Benedictum sit nomen Dei."

ANTONIUS STRADIUARIUS, OF CREMONA.

Case IX.

BUTLER, Mr. FRANK H.—*Violin*, Italian, by Antonius Stradiuarius, of Cremona. Date 1709.

ARKWRIGHT, Mr. J. H.—*Violin*, Italian, by Antonius Stradiuarius, of Cremona. Date 1732.

JOHNSON, Miss E.—*Violin*, Italian, by Antonius Stradiuarius, of Cremona. Date 1698.

JOHNSON, Miss M. E.—*Violin*, Italian, by Antonius Stradiuarius, of Cremona. Date 1721.

CURTEIS, Rev. T. S.—*Violin*, of the "long pattern," Italian, by Antonius Stradiuarius, of Cremona. Date 1692. From the Earl of Falmouth's Collection.

OLDAKER, Mr. T.—*Violin*, Italian, by Antonius Stradiuarius. From the Earl of Falmouth's Collection.

BOOTH, Herr OTTO VON.—*Violin*, Italian, by Antonius Stradiuarius. 1715.

SEILLIÉRE M. le Baron F.—*Violin*, Italian, by Antonius Stradiuarius of Cremona. Date 1672.

A specimen of his earliest period (called Amatisée) formerly in the possession of Paganini and afterwards of Mdlle. Carolina Ferni.

YEO, Mr. H. VIVIAN.—*Violin*, Italian, by Antonius Stradiuarius, of Cremona. Date 1704.

Case X.

HILL, Messrs. W. E., & SONS.—*Viola*, by Antonius Stradiuarius, of Cremona. A perfect specimen of the "late period." Date 1721.
—— A collection of old bows of 17th and 18th century. Most of the sticks made of snake wood. The progress from the long-pointed head to the present form will be observed.

TYRELL, Mr. A.—*Viola.* A perfect specimen of the "early period." Italian, by Antonius Stradiuarius, of Cremona. Date 1690.

HARRISON. Mr. R. L.—*Violin bow,* by the elder Tourte.
—— *Violin Bow,* by François Tourte. This bow belonged to Kiesewetter.

HILL, Messrs. W. E., & SONS.—*Violin,* Italian. by Antonius Stradiuarius, of Cremona. A perfect specimen of the "late period." Date 1732.
—— *Bow.* One of the earliest types.

CROALL, Mr. WILLIAM.—*Violin,* Italian, by Antonius Stradiuarius, of Cremona. Date 1716.

From the "Cessol Collection," and formerly the property of the violinist Artot. A perfect specimen of the "Grand pattern."

—— *Violin,* Italian, by Antonius Stradiuarius, of Cremona. Date 1711.

From the Fountaine and Plowden Collections. An equally fine specimen of the "Grand pattern."

ARDITI, Signor LUIGI.—*Violin,* Italian, by Antonius Stradiuarius, of Cremona. A very fine specimen of the early period. Date 1689.

ASHBURNHAM, Earl of.—An old fluted bow.

Wall Case.

DALE, Mr. WILLIAM.—*Spinet,* by Charles Haward. About 1660. See Pepy's 'Diary' and Grove's 'Dictionary' concerning Haward.

SACCHI, Mr. FREDERICO.—*Guitar,* Roman, two necks and twelve strings. About 1840.
—— *Guitar,* Cremona. 1803.

GROVE, Sir GEORGE.—*Spinet,* English, by Stephen Keene. About 1700.

HIPKINS, Mr. A. J.—Diagram of Sir George Grove's *Spinet,* by R. Maitland.

LEHMANN, Mr. RUDOLF.—*Chitarrone,* Venetian.

VINNICOMBE, Mr. W.—*Spinet,* by Edward Blount. 1664.

Has the autograph of Thomas Hitchcock, as maker, on a key and on the jacks. Double sharps in the bass.

HILL, Messrs. W. E., & SONS.—*Violin case,* German. About 1700.
—— *Violin case,* English. 18th century.

HUGHES, Mr. E. R.—*Spinet*, English, by Stephen Keene. 1706.

SMITH, Mr. HUBERT.—Malibran's *Guitar*.
This guitar was made for Madame Malibran. She died in 1836.

VEASEY, Mr. R. G.—*Cavaquinto.* A small guitar, used only in the Western Isles. Brought from St. Michael's in 1845.

PRATTEN, Madame SIDNEY.—*Guitar*, English. 1832.
—— *Terz Guitar.* 1832.
—— Two *Gigelire* (wooden harmonicons).

CHESTER, Mr. JOHN.—*Guitar*, Portuguese. 18th century.

KENNEDY, Mr. E. H.—*Dital Harp.*

PAYNE, Mr. E. J.—*Viola da Gamba*, English, by Henry Key, of Southwark, London. Date 1611.

.—*Viola d'Amore.*

—— *Bijuga Cither.*
—— *Viol.*

OAKELEY, Sir HERBERT.—Keyed *Cither.*

GLEN, Messrs. J. & R.—Keyed *Cither.*

PAYNE, Mr. E. J.—*Viola da Gamba*, English, by Barak Norman of London. Date about 1715.

HORSLEY, Mr. W. C.—*Dital Harp.* Early 19th century.

CHESTER, Mr. JOHN.— *Lute*, convolvulus pattern. 17th century.

DECCA, Mdlle. MARIE.—*Guitar*, tortoiseshell and mother of pearl. 18th century.

.—*Guitar.*

Small Wall Case.

CHESTER, Mr. JOHN.—Dresden china figures of Musicians, &c.

PICTURE.

SPENCER, Earl. — 44. Portrait of Sofonisba Anguisciola playing the Spinet, painted by herself.

DIVISION 5.

Case XI.

LAMOUREUX, Mons. CHARLES.—*Violin*, Italian. By Antonius Stradiuarius. Date 1722. Formerly belonged to Rode.

HILL, Mr. W. H.—*Viola Bow*, French, by Tourte.

MOUNTFORD, Mr. J.—*Violin Bow*, French, by Tourte. Date about 1790.

PERKIN, Mr. T. Dix.—*Viola Bow*, English, by Dodd.
—— *Violin Bow*, by François Tourte (round stick).
——   ”   ”   ”   ”   (octagonal stick).
—— *Violoncello Bow*, French, by Tourte. 18th century.
—— *Violin*, Italian, by Antonius Stradiuarius, of Cremona. Date 1718.

PARMENTIER, Madame.—*Violin*, Italian, by Antonius Stradiuarius. Date 1728.

This was formerly the property of Dragonetti, who bequeathed it at his death in 1846 to Térésa Milanollo, now the wife of M le General Parmentier.

COURTAULD, Mr. SYDNEY.—*Violin*, Italian, by Antonius Stradiuarius, of Cremona. Date 1734. Interesting on account of its date being made when Stradiuarius had reached the age of 84 or 85.

ORCHAR, Mr. JAMES G.—*Violin*, Italian, by Antonius Stradiuarius, of Cremona. Date 1714. A very fine specimen of the "Grand pattern." From the Adam Collection.

YEO, Mr. H. VIVIAN —*Violin Bow*, Old French.

Formerly "De Beriot's." Given him by his master Robberechts. On the nut, original inscription, "Ayant appartenu a Robberechts. C. de B."

HILL, Messrs. W. E., & Sons.—Three *Violin Bows*, English. By the elder Dodd.

HEATHCOTE, Mr. W. E.—*Violin*, Italian, by Antonius Stradiuarius, of Cremona. Date 1701.

C

CROMPTON, Mr. GEORGE. — *Violin*, Italian, by Antonius Stradiuarius, of Cremona. Date 1679.

Finely inlaid on the sides and scroll. Ornamental purfling. Called "The Helier" Stradiuarius, having been purchased about the year 1734 by Sir Samuel Helier of Wombourne, in whose family it remained until recently, when it was bought by the present owner.

BORWICK, Mr. ALFRED.—*Violoncello Bow*, French, by Tourte.

For many years attached to the Stradiuarius violoncello of General Olivers, now the solo instrument of Signor Piatti.

JOSEPH GUARNERIUS DEL GESU AND ANDREA GUARNERIUS.

Case XII.

KINGHORN, Mr. J. M.—*Violin*, Italian, by Joseph Guarnerius del Gesu, of Cremona. Date 1739.

McGOWAN, Mr. JOHN.—*Viola*, Italian, by Andrea Guarnerius, of Cremona. Date 1676. From the collection of the late Sir Wm. Curtis, Bart.
—— *Viola*, Italian, by Joseph Guarnerius del Gesu, of Cremona. Date 1742. Brought from Italy by Tarisio, formerly the Violin of Meerts of the Brussels Conservatoire.

ELPHINSTONE, Colonel Sir HOWARD.—*Violin*, Italian, by Joseph Guarnerius del Gesu, of Cremona. Date 1734. Formerly the property of the violinist Spagnoletti.

HEATH, Mr. H. B.—*Violin*, Italian, by Joseph Guarnerius del Gesu, of Cremona. Date 1742. From the Plowden Collection.

.ORCHAR, Mr. J. G.—*Violin*, Italian, by Joseph Guarnerius del Gesu, of Cremona. 1738. From the Adam collection.

HILL, Messrs. W. E., & SONS.—*Violin*, Italian. By Joseph Guarnerius del Gesu, of Cremona. Date 1740.

LEHMANN, Mr. F.—*Violin*, Italian, by Joseph Guarnerius del Gesu, of Cremona. Date 1727. Brought to England by Ole Bull, afterwards in the Goding and Plowden collections.

HIPKINS, Mr. A. J.—*Violin*, Italian. By Petrus Guarnerius of Mantua. Date 1701.

THE VENETIAN SCHOOL.

Case XIII.

BORWICK, Mr. ALFRED.—*Violoncello*, Italian, by Dominico Montagnana, of Venice. About 1700. For many years in the collection of the late King of Bavaria.

HEATH, Mr. H. B.—*Violin*, Italian, by Petrus Guarnerius, of Venice. From the Gillott Collection.
—— *Violoncello*, Ital an, by Sanctus Seraphin, of Venice. Date about 1730. Called "The Beauty" on account of its very handsome wood.

GORTON, Mr. STEWART. — *Violoncello*, by Dominicus Montagnana. About 1700.

EDWARDS, Mr. W.—*Violin*, Italian, by Sanctus Seraphin, of Venice. Date 1743.

WITHERS, Mr. G.—*Violin*, Italian. By Carlo Tononius, of Venice. Date 1722.

AMATI, RUGGERIUS AND JOSEPH GUARNERIUS FILIUS ANDREAE.

Case XIV.

HILL, Messrs W. E., & SONS.—*Violin*, by Joseph Guarnerius filius Andreae, Cremona. About 1700.

MACKENZIE, Dr. G. W.—*Violin*, Italian, by Joseph Guarnerius filius Andreae. 1714.

For many years the solo instrument of the well-known violinist, Mr. J. T. Carrodus. The specimen of the maker referred to and illustrated by Mr. G. Hart in his work on the Violin and its Makers.

JOY, Mr. EDWARD.—*Violoncello*, Italian, by Antonius and Hieronymus Amati, of Cremona. Date 1642.

Brought from Italy by Giardini. Afterwards in the possession (amongst others) of George IV., Robert Lindley, Sir Wm. Curtis, Bart., and General Oliver.

COURTAULD, Mr. SYDNEY.—*Violin*, Italian, by Joseph Guarnerius filius Andreae. Date 1709.

JOHNSON, Mr. DAVID.—*Violoncello*, Italian, by Francesco Ruggerius, of Cremona. Date 1672.

c 2

BRIDGES, Rev. ALEXANDER H.—*Violoncello*, Italian, by Andreas Amatus, of Cremona. Date 1572.

Presented by Pope Pius V. to Charles IX. of France. Called "The King." The instrument referred to by Forster and Sandys in their History of the Violin (page 203).

Wall Case.

WELLESLEY, Mr. GERALD E.—*Clavichord*, japanned case. 1763.

PYNE, Mr. KENDRICK.—*Clavichord*, decorated. Brought from Germany by the late Carl Engel.

————.—*Tromba Marina*, or (German) *Trumschei.*

———— *Hurdy Gurdy.* " " "
———— *Dital Harp.*

CRAMER, Messrs. J. B., & Co.—*Clavichord*, by Hass, decorated. Anno 1743.

HUGHES, Mr. E. R.—*Clavichord* (Gebunden, *i.e.*, two notes to one pair of strings).

CHESTER, Mr. JOHN.—*Guitar*, diamond shaped rose, Spanish. 18th century.

GLEN, Messrs. J. & R.—*Cither.*

BRUTON, Mr. S.—*Guitar*, Neapolitan. Date 1790.

.—*Lute.*

WILMOTT, Miss E. A.—*Mandoline*, Neapolitan.

EXETER, Marquess of.—*Cither*, ten stringed.

DECCA, Mdlle. MARIE.—*Mandoline.* 18th century.

WYBARD, Mr. F. J.—*Harp-Lute*, seven stringed. English. 18th century.

DECCA, Mdle. MARIE.—*Mandoline.* Spanish. 18th century.

.—*Mandoline*, Neapolitan.
———— *Lute.*

GLEN, Messrs. J. & R.—*Lute.*

DECCA, Mdlle. MARIE.—*Guitar*, Neapolitan, by C. Battista.
———— *Mandoline*, Italian. 1760.
———— *Bijuga Cither.* 1760.

CHESTER, Mr. JOHN.—*Machete,* or small *Guitar,* the frets noted by numbers, Portuguese. 18th century.

.— *Double-necked Guitar.*

———

MAHILLON & Co., Messrs.—*Drum.* Relic of Waterloo, 18th June, 1815. 7th or Queen's Own Hussars.

PICTURE.

OXFORD, UNIVERSITY OF.—45. Portrait of Bernard Gates.

DIVISION 6.

Techler, Montagnana and Guadagnini.

Case XV.

Harvie, Mr. Edgar C.—*Violoncello*, Italian, by David Techler, of Rome. Date 1714.

Johnson, Mr. David.—*Violin*, by Jo. Baptista Guadagnini. Turin, 1785.
—— *Violoncello*, Italian, by Dominicus Montagnana, of Venice. Date about 1700.

Piatti, Signor.—*Violin*, by Joannes Baptista Guadagnini, fecit Cremonæ. 1748.

Hill, Mr. W. H.—*Viola*, by Joannes Baptista Guadagnini. 1747.

Shuttleworth, Mr. T. M.—*Violoncello*, Italian, by David Techler of Rome. Date about 1700.

The Dutch and German Schools.

Case XVI.

Hill, Messrs. W. E., & Sons.—*Violoncello*, by Carlo Ferdinandus Landulphus. Milan. Date 1761.
—— *Violin*, Dutch School, maker unknown.
—— *Violin*, Dutch, by Hendrik Jacobs of Amsterdam. Date 1693.
—— ,, ,, by Hendrik Jacobs, of Amsterdam. Date about 1690. After the style of Amati.

Battersby, Mr. N.—*Violin*, German, by Jacobus Stainer. Date 1671.

Matthew, Mr. James E.—*Violin*, German, by Jacobus Stainer, of Absam. Date 1652.

SANDEMAN, Mr. E. A.—*Violoncello*, Dutch, by Peter Rombouts, of Amsterdam. Date 1720.

ALARD, Mons. DELPHIN.— *Violin*, German, by Jacobus Stainer, of Amsterdam. Date 1679.

STRADIUARIUS AND HIS PUPIL CARLO BERGONZI.

Case XVII.

HARRISON, Mr. DARENT.—*Violoncello,* Italian, by Carlo Bergonzi, of Cremona. Date 1734.

ISAAC, Mr. J. SWINTON.—*Violoncello*, Italian, by Antonius Stradiuarius, of Cremona. Date 1711.

Brought to England by Mara, husband of Madame Mara. Sold by him to Mr. Crosdil, who sold it at the beginning of the present century to General Bosville, afterwards Lord Macdonald. His son disposed of it to Mr. Lucas, who played on it for some time at the Italian Opera, and subsequently parted with it to Mr. G. Whitmore Isaac.

HEATH, Mr. H. B.—*Violin*, Italian, by Carlo Bergonzi, of Cremona. Date 1727.

PERKIN, Mr. THOMAS DIX.—*Violoncello*, Italian, by Antonius Stradiuarius. 1624.

From Sir William Curtis's and the Goding Collections. Said to have been made by Stradiuarius for a Corflote nobleman, and deposited by him in a chest with cotton and there left for at least a century.

—— *Violin*, Italian, by Carlo Bergonzi, of Cremona. Date about 1735.

GURNEY, Mr. H. G.—*Violin*, Italian, by Carlo Bergonzi, of Cremona. Date 1730. The back and sides of beech.

Wall Case.

PYNE, Mr. KENDRICK.—*Dulcimer*, decorated.
—— *Spinet*, probably by Keene.

KLINCKERFUSS, Herr.—*Dulcimer*. 1757.

DALE, Mr. H. J.—*Spinet*, by Stephen Keene. About 1700.

BONHAM, Mr. W. W.—*Dulcimer*.

LAVINO, Mr. W.—*Japanese Koto*.

.—*Violoncello*.
—— *Viol*.
—— *Violoncello*, curious shape.
—— *Viol*.

.—*Viola da Gamba.*
—— *Tenor Viol.*
—— *Viola da Gamba.*
—— *Treble Viol.*
—— *Viola da Gamba.*
—— *Tenor Viol.*
—— *Viola da Gamba.*

——

LE STRANGE, Mr. HAMON.—*Chamber Organ.* About 1660.

PICTURES, ETC.

DOWDESWELL & DOWDESWELL, Messrs. — 46. Portrait of
Richard Wagner, etched by H. Herkomer.
—— 47. Richard Wagner at Bayreuth. Photograph from a
drawing by G. Papperitz.

SQUIRE, Mr. W. B.—46*a.* Autograph Letter of Richard
Wagner.

ELLA, Professor, 47*a.* Original MS. of portion of Wagner's
Tannhäuser, and photograph of the composer.

OXFORD, UNIVERSITY OF.—48. Portrait of John Hingston.

DIVISION 7.

FIELDING, Major-General the Hon. PERCY, C.B.—*Euphonicon,* Stewart's Patent. About 1840.

Cox, Mr. CORNELIUS.—*Grand Piano,* by John Broadwood & Sons. Wedgwood plaques and Tassie medallions. London, 1798.

Wall Stand.

MARSHALL, Mr. JULIAN.—Portrait of Verdi, by Geoffrey.
—— Autograph Letter of Verdi. 1856.
—— „ „ „ 1846.
—— Portrait of Buchinger, drawn by himself.
—— „ Lablache, by Brown, after Tatham.
—— Autograph Letter of Lablache. 1828.
—— Portrait of Angelica Catalani. 1807.
—— Ticket, signed by Angelica Catalani.
—— Articles of Agreement for the first engagement in England, of Madame Catalini, 26th Oct., 1805.
—— Autograph Letter of Madame Pasta. 1821.
—— Portrait of Madame Pasta, by Hayger.
—— „ Staudigl.
—— Autograph Letter of Staudigl. 1851.
—— Portrait of Belcke (the Paganini of the Trombone).
—— Original Manuscript by Belcke. Berlin, 1848.
—— Autograph Letter of Haydn to La Polzelli.
—— Original Manuscript by Haydn (Quartett).
—— Portrait of Owen MacSwiney, by Faber, after Vanloo. 1752.
—— Autograph Letter from Owen MacSwiney to Colley Cibber. 1706.
—— Portrait of Dr. Burney, by Bartolozzi, after Sir Joshua Reynolds.
—— Portrait of Spohr, by Geoffroy.
—— Autograph Letter of Spohr. 1835.
—— Portrait of Graun, by Preisler.

MARSHALL, Mr. JULIAN.—Portrait of Duport (Violoncello). Crayon drawing.
—— Portrait of Duport (smaller).
—— „ Romberg.
—— Original Manuscript by Romberg, 'Andante,' for viol ncello.
—— Portrait of Lowe (organist), by Becket, after Hays.
—— „ Hasse, by Zucchi, after Rotari.
—— „ Britton (small coal man and musician), engraved by J. Johnson.
—— Portrait of Johann Strauss.
—— Original Manuscript by Strauss.
—— Portrait of Mrs. Billington as St. Cecilia, after Joshua Reynolds.
—— Letter of Mrs. Billington, dated 1809.
—— Autograph Letter of Signora Storace. 1816.
—— Portrait of Signora Storace. 1788.
—— Ticket signed by Storace. 1790.
—— Portrait of Guiletta Grisi, by Hamerton, after Deveria. 1835.
—— Autograph Letter of Madame Grisi. 1856.
—— Articles of Agreement between Laporte and Rubini. 1833.
—— Portrait of Haydn, by Schiavonetti, after Gruntenbrunn.
—— Portrait of Rameau (composer), by Prévost, after Garaud.
—— Portrait of Rameau (composer), by Delatre.
—— „ Viotti (composer and violinist), by Cardon, after Chinery.
—— Coloured Print. Caricature of Handel, after Goupy.
—— Portrait of Paisiello, by Beissan, after Le Brun.
—— Caricature of Handel, after Goupy.
—— Portrait of Madame Mara, by Collyer, after Jean.
—— Autograph Letter of Madame Mara, dated 1793.
—— Portrait of Ole Bornemann Bull (violinist).
—— Autograph Letter of Ole Bull.

EXETER, Marquess of.—*Eolichord*, or *Æolian harp* made by Longman and Broderip.

PICTURES, ETC.

ELLIS, Mr. W. F.—49. "Apollo."   By Pietro Benvenuti.
1805.

DICEY, Mr. FRANK.—50. Portrait of B. Hollander, by the
Lender.

HILL, Mr. A. G.—51. Organ at Jutfaas, near Utrecht, being
a plate from 'The Organ Cases and Organs of the
Middle Ages and Renaissance.' By the Lender.

OXFORD, UNIVERSITY OF.—52. Portrait of James Hestletine.

DIVISION 8.

Case XVIII.

CHIMAY, Prince J. de Caraman.
—— Two *Violins*, *Viola* and *Violoncello*, ornamented with pictures and a carved head, also inscribed, modern French, by J. B. Vuillaume. Date 1865. Copy of Stradiuarius.

GAND, M. EUGENE. — *Viole d'Amour*, French, by Nicolas Lupot. The only one he made. Date 1817.
—— *Viola*, French, by the brothers Adolphe and Eugène Gand. Date 1859.

Bears the arms of Napoleon III. and is a reproduction of one of the instruments of the Royal Chapel, destroyed in 1871 by the conflagration at the Tuileries.

—— *Violin*, French, made by C. F. Gand. Date 1829.
—— *Viola*, French, by C. F. Gand (son-in-law of Lupot). Date 1825.

This instrument was made for the chapel of King Charles X., and was broken on the 29th July, 1830, when the Tuileries were invaded by the insurgents. The belly was restored with fragments of other instruments destroyed at the same time.

POLLITZER, Mr. A.—*Violin*, inlaid and ornamented with stones, etc., modern French, by J. B. Vuillaume. Date about 1850. Reproduction of a Nicolaus Amatus. Original in the collection of Prince Youssoupow.

Case XIX.

HILL, Messrs. W. E., & SONS.—*Violoncello*, English, Joseph Hill, maker, at the Harp and Flute in the Haymarket. Date 1770.
—— *Violoncello*, English, by William Forster, sen. Amati copy. Date about 1780.

PIATTI, Signor.—*Violoncello*, English, by Betts. Copy of the Andreas Amatus. Presented by Pope Pius to Charles IX. of France. Painting on back and Latin inscription on the sides.

Case XX.

BONJOUR, MONS. A. — *Violoncello*, Italian, by Antonius Stradiuarius. Date 1691.

—— *Violoncello*, Italian, by Franciscus Ruggerius. Date 1695.

—— *Violoncello*, Italian, by Antonius Stradiuarius. Date 1689.

Formerly one of the celebrated quartet of Stradiuarius instruments in the collection of the Count Archinto, of Milan.

—— Three *Violoncello Bows*, French (one with gold and tortoise-shell mountings), by Tourte.

TAUDOU, MONS.—*Violin*, Italian, by Petrus Guarnerius. Date 1695.

PARMENTIER, MADAME.—*Violin*, Italian, by Gaspar di Salo of Brescia. Date about 1580. Formerly the property of Dragonetti, who bequeathed it to Maria Milanollo.

Wall Case.

THE CONSERVATOIRE ROYAL OF BRUSSELS.—*Basson Russe*, by C. Sax, of Brussels.

—— *Bassoon*, with three rotary cylinders, adapted to an ophicleide body, showing one of the first transformations of the instrument.

—— *Slide Trombone*, by W. Magnus, of Nuremburg.

—— *Serpent*, by Embach, of Amsterdam. About 1830.

—— *Trumpet*, with two valves, by C. Sax, of Brussels. One of the first adaptations of the pistons.

—— *Trumpet*, by Johannes Wilhelm, of Nuremburg.

—— „ by Johannes Wilhelm, of Nuremburg.

—— „ by Johannes Wilhelm, of Nuremburg. 1694.

—— „ curved in half circles for using the stopped notes.

—— *Basset Horn*, curved in a half circle. English.

—— *Trombone*, by Hans Heimer, of Nuremburg. 1668.

—— *Basset Horn*. Signed " Papaline."

—— *Trombone*, by Tuerlincks of Malines. End of 18th century.

—— *Basson Russe*, by Snider, of Lyons.

—— *Clavichord*, Flemish, Gebunden. 17th century.

—— *Dulcimer*, French.

—— *Upright Grand Pianoforte*, by Frederici of Gera, 1745. (See engraving of the action, by John Hipkins, on screen.)

JOURET, Mons. LEON.—*Virginal*, by Hans Ruckers. 1628.

MABILLON, Mons. VICTOR.—*Great Bass Flute.* 16th century.
—— *Great Bass Flute.*
—— *Lituus* of the Roman Cavalry.
—— *Buccino* of the Roman Infantry.
—— *Clavecin*, by Hans Ruckers.
—— *Regale*, with two bellows, of the end of the 16th century. Played upon at the Historic Concerts I. I. E.

PICTURE.

OXFORD, UNIVERSITY OF.—53. Portrait of Dr. Pepusch.

DIVISION 9.

Case XXI.

CHIMAY, PRINCE J. DE CARAMAN.—Two *Violins*, a *Viola* and a *Violoncello*, Belgian, by Ambroise De Comble, of Tournay, supposed to have been a pupil of Stradiuarius. Date about 1750.

ANDREOLI, SIGNOR C.—*Viola*, modern Italian, by Giacomo Rivolta, of Milan. Date 1822.
—— *Violin*, modern Italian, by Joannes Franciscus Pressenda, of Turin. Date 1830.

CROMPTON, Mr. W.—*Violin*, Italian, by Camillus Camilli, of Mantua. Date 1739.

WITHERS, Mr. G.—*Viola*, by Giovanni Grancino, of Milan. Ornamentation round purfling.

JOHNSON, Mr. D.—*Viola*, Italian, by Laurentius Storioni, of Cremona. Date about 1780.

WARNER, Mr. W. P.—*Violin*, Italian, by Joannes Franciscus Pressenda. Turin, 1843.

Case XXII.

.—*Ivory Guitar*, Italian.
—— *Treble Lute.*
—— ” ”
—— *Mandoline.*
—— ” Milanese.

HILL, Messrs. W. E., & SONS.—*Guitar*, Italian, by Antonius Stradiuarius. Date 1680. Probably the only guitar known made by Stradiuarius. Brought from Brescia.

ALARD, Mons. DELPHIN.—*Cetera*, Italian, by Antonius Stradiuarius. Date 1700. Beautifully carved.

Case XXIII.

D'EGVILLE, Mr. LOUIS HERVEY, Junr.—*Violin*, by Nicolas Lupot, copy of Joseph Guaruerius. Date about 1800.

BELBEUF, LA MARQUISE. — *Violin*, French, by Nicolas Médard, of Nancy. Date 1655.

SEILLIÈRE, BARON F.—*Violin*, French, by F. L. Pique. Date 1796.

Formerly the property of Rodolphe Kreutzer, Auguste Kreutzer, and Massart, Professors of the Paris Conservatoire.

WITHERS, Mr. G.—*Violin*, French, by Nicolas Lupot, of Paris. Date 1823.

GAND, Mons. EUGÈNE.—*Violin*, French, made at Orleans by François Lupot, the father of Nicolas Lupot, 1771.
—— *Violin*, French, by Nicolas Lupot. Date 1814.

RICHARDSON, Rev. JOHN. — *Violin*, French, by Nicolas Lupot. Date about 1790. A specimen of his early work, made at Orleans.

DELOR, Madame.—*Violin*, French, by Nicolas Lupot. Date 1798.
—— Miniature *Violin*.
—— *Pochette*.

Wall Case.

THE BRUSSELS CONSERVATOIRE.—*Clavecin*, with double keyboard, by Hieronymus Hass. Hamburg, 1734.
—— *Clavecin brisé*, or folding *Spinet*, by Marius. Paris, 1709.
—— *Clavecin*, with double keyboard. Signed "Tibaut à Tolose, 1679."
—— *Virginal*, by Georgius Britsen, of Antwerp. 1686.
—— *Tromba Marina*. Signed " F. Honyer Nanner."
—— *Viola da Gamba*. Played by Mons. Jacobs in the Historic Concerts, I. I. E. *Sympathetic strings*.
—— *Viola da Gamba*.
—— *Rebab and bow*.

DALE, Mr. WILLIAM.—*Spinet*, by Thomas Barton. 1730, London.

PICTURE.

OXFORD, UNIVERSITY OF.—54. Portrait of Thomas Blagrave.

DIVISION 10.

Case XXIIIa.

PAYNE, Mr. E. J.—*Viola da Gamba*, English, by Henry Key, of Southwark. Date 1611. In original condition.
—— *Viola da Gamba*, English, by Barak Norman. Date about 1715.
—— *Quinton* or *Pardessus de Viole* (treble viol), French, by Ludovicus Guersan, of Paris. Date 1763.

LENDET, MONS. LEON.—*Viola d'Amore*, Italian, by Ferdinando Gugliano, of Naples. Date 1763.

.—*Viol d'Amore.*

Case XXIV.

MOUGENOT, MONS. GEORGES.
—— *Mandoline*, Neapolitan.

—— ,,   ,,
—— *Mandora.*
—— *Viole d'Amour.*
—— *Guitar.*
—— *Cistre.*
—— *Pochette.*

Case XXV.

CONSERVATOIRE ROYAL OF BRUSSELS. — *Spinet*, Italian. Signed " Antoni Patavini Opus, M.D.XXXXX."

Case XXVI.

Lord TOLLEMACHE, of Helmingham.—*Queen Elizabeth's Lute.*

This instrument (which is known by the above title) is said to have been left by Queen Elizabeth in 1584, at Helmingham Hall, Suffolk, as a heirloom to commemorate Her Majesty having stood sponsor to an infant, who was after Sir Lyonel Tollemache, Knight, M.P. for Suffolk. The label within is as follows: " Johannes Rosa, Londini, fecit. In Bridwell the 27th of July, 1580." Round the rim is inscribed in inlaid letters, " Cymbalum decachordon, 1580." The lute has never left Helmingham until it was lent for exhibition here, and, in all probability (judging from its fine condition), has scarcely ever been removed from its case. In any case this is the work of John Rose, the Inventor of the pandore or orpheoreon mentioned by Prætorius, and it compares for beauty of design and work with the cetera in an adjacent case by Stradiuarius.

Wall Case.

The Conservatoire Royal of Brussels. — *Orchestral Flute*, by T. G. Trever, of Potsdam. It has eight keys and three different pieces for the upper part, and one other piece for the lower part.

—— *Spinet*, Flemish. Painting inside the lid.

—— „ attributed to Marius of Paris.

—— Collection of Six Bows, of various dates.

—— *Orgue Portatif*, or *Regale*, Italian. 17th century; a very rare instrument, only two known to exist.

—— *Bettelleier*, or *Hurdy Gurdy*, German.

—— *Vielle*, by Cesar Pons, of Grenoble. About 1790.

—— *Orchestral Flute*, ivory, with three extra pieces.

—— *Harpanetta*. or *Spitzharfe*. Double sounding board.

—— Two *Bass Flutes*, 16th century.

—— *Orgue Positif*. 17th century. Played on at the Historic Concerts I. I. E.

—— *Keyed Cither*.

—— *Viol*, Neapolitan.

—— *Oud*, Old Egyptian.

—— *Nine-Stringed Lyre-Guitar*, French.

—— *Theorbo*. Signed " Joannes Storino, fecit, Anno Domino 1725."

—— *Mandora*, Italian.

—— *Guitar*, Italian.

—— *Bijuga-Cither*, signed by Renault et Chatelaine.

—— *Violin*, Norwegian.

—— *Viola* (tenor), by Johann Christian Hoffmaan, said to have belonged to J. S. Bach, signed Matteu Selles.

—— *Keyed Cither*, English.

—— *Cither*, by Limbertas Niggell. 1761.

—— *Viola da Gamba*, by Joachim Tielke, of Hamburg. 1701.

—— *Mandoline*.

—— *Viole d'Amour*, by Solomon.

—— *Viol* (treble), German. 1688.

—— *Viol*, made of canes, Sicilian.

—— *Rebec*, Italian.

—— *Viole d'Amour*, seven strings.

—— *Pardessus de Viole*, by Gerard J. de la Blanque.

—— *Viola da Gamba*, made in 1596.

—— *Cither*, by De la Blanque, of Lisle.

—— *Viol* (treble), by Nicholas Mevaer. 1700.

—— *Guitar*, Italian.

—— *Bijuga-Cither*.—London. 1766.

—— *Guitar Lyre*.

—— *Mandora*, Neapolitan.

THE CONSERVATOIRE ROYAL OF BRUSSELS. — *Viola di Bardone.*
—— *Cither*, Polish.

PICTURE.

OXFORD, UNIVERSITY OF.—55. Portrait of J. P. Salamon.

DIVISION 11.

MAHILLON, Mons. VICTOR.—*Harpsichord*, by Burkat Shudi and Johannes Broadwood. 1773. Belonged to the Empress Maria Theresa.

PICTURES, ETC.

OXFORD, UNIVERSITY OF.—56. Portrait of Handel.

MUSICIANS, ROYAL SOCIETY OF.—57. Portrait of Handel.
—— 58. Portrait of Handel. The gift of Redmond Simpson, Esq., to the Royal Society of Musicians.

The Rev. Sir FREDERICK GORE-OUSELEY, Bart.
—— 59. Dr. J. Blow, by Sir Peter Lely.
—— 60. Portrait of Purcell. The gift of Redmond Simpson, Esq. Lent by the Royal College of Music to the Royal Society of Musicians.

MARSHALL, MR. JULIAN.
—— 61. Engraving. Portrait of Handel.

MUSIC, ROYAL ACADEMY OF.—62. John Fane, 6th Earl of Westmoreland, founder of the Royal Academy of Music, 1784–1859. Painted by Mrs. L. Goodman.

WITHERS, Mr. EDWARD.—63. George III. playing the Flute, Giardini playing the Violin, Lord Aylesford playing the Violoncello.

LITTLETON, Mr. HENRY.—64. Portrait of Handel, by Denner.

THE FITZWILLIAM MUSEUM, CAMBRIDGE.—65. G. F. Handel. Painted by Sir James Thornhill.
—— 66. Small Portrait of Handel.
—— 67. Autograph Letter of Handel's.

CUMMINGS, Mr. W.—68. Handel (Portrait of), by Francis Kyte. 1742.

MACKENZIE, Mrs.—69. Portrait of Neil Gow, by Sir Henry Raeburn.

MUSIC, ROYAL ACADEMY OF.—70. William Crotch, Mus. D., Oxon (as a boy), Professor of Music in the University of Oxford, and first Principal of the Royal Academy of Music, 1757–1847. Painted by George Romney.

CASE, Mr. THOMAS—71. Portrait of Robert Bennett, by Wageman.

OXFORD, UNIVERSITY OF.—72. Portrait of William Lawes.

DIVISION 12.

Case XXVIa.

CUMMINGS, Mr. W. H.—*Lace Ruffle*, worn by Handel.
—— *Handel's Will.*
—— *Inventory* of Handel's goods, taken after his death.

H.M. THE QUEEN.—Handel, G. F., 'Messiah,' full score, in the handwriting of J. C. Smith. Folio, 1741.
—— Handel, G. F., 'Messiah,' full score, autograph. The original manuscript.
—— Handel, G. F., 'Dettingen Te Deum,' full score. Folio, autograph, 1743.
—— Handel, G. F., 'Israel in Egypt,' full score. Folio, autograph, 1738.
—— Handel, G. F., 'Alcina,' full score. Ob. folio, autograph, 1735.

OUSELEY, The Rev. Sir F. A. Gore, Bart.—Handel, G. F., 'The Messiah.'

Full score, mostly in the handwriting of J. C. Smith (Handel's amanuensis), but containing many corrections, &c., and three entire songs in Handel's autograph. It was from this copy that Handel conducted the first performance of the Oratorio. About 1741. 2 vols. Ob. folio.

HIPKINS, Mr. A. J.—Handel's Suite de Pièces, original edition, with the Composer's preface.

DRIFFIELD, Rev. G. T.—*Handel's Tuning-fork.* 1749.
—— *A Tenor Fork.* About 1715.

LITTLETON, Mr. HENRY.—Statue of Handel, by Roubiliac, formerly at Vauxhall Gardens.

CASE, Mr. THOMAS.—*Spinet*, by Thomas Hitchcock. Early 18th century. Formerly belonging to Sir Sterndale Bennett.

PICTURES.

TAPHOUSE, Mr. T. W.—73. Gustavus Waltz, by J. M. Hauck.

LITTLETON, Mr. HENRY.—74. Joah Bates and his Wife, by F. Coates, R.A.

CASE, Mr. THOMAS.—75. Sir Sterndale Bennett, by Sir J. E. Millais, Bart., R.A.

OXFORD, UNIVERSITY OF.—76. Portrait of Orlando Gibbons.
—— 77. Portrait of Corelli.
—— 78. Portrait of Robert Hudson.
—— 79. Portrait of John Wilson.
—— 80. Portrait of
—— 81. Portrait of

HILDITCH, Miss MARY.—82. Three Sisters, one playing a Spinet, by Gainsborough.

BROWN, Mr. J. J.—Choir of a Spanish Cathedral, by E. Long, R.A.

OXFORD, UNIVERSITY OF.—84. Portrait of Henry Lawes.

DAVY, Mr. G. B.—84A. Portrait of Mozart, by Battoni.

DIVISION 13.

PICTURES.

OXFORD, UNIVERSITY OF.—85. Portrait of William Heather.

LEFEVRE, Mr. L. H.—86. The Singing Class, by A. Ludovici, Jun.

PAWLE, Mr. F. C.—87. Portrait of Alfredo Piatti, by Frank Holl, R.A.

SELLE, Dr.—88. Portrait of Stewart (Violinist), by Wright.

BROWN, Mr. J. J.—89. "The Impromptu Dance," by F. Brown.

OXFORD, UNIVERSITY OF.—90. Portrait of Lord Crewe.

SWEARS, Mr. HENRY.—91. "The Dancing Class," by A. Ludovici, Jun.

MUSICIANS, ROYAL SOCIETY OF.—92. Portrait of Thomas Molyneux.

OXFORD, UNIVERSITY OF.—93. Portrait of Sir John Hawkins.

ALLEN, Mr. E. H.—94. Portrait of J. B. Viotti, by Madame Le Brun.

OXFORD, UNIVERSITY OF.—95. Portrait of Dr. Burney.

BROADWOOD & SONS, Messrs. JOHN.—96. Rehearsal of an Opera. Attributed to Sebastian Ricci.

OXFORD, UNIVERSITY OF.—97. Portrait of Dr. Gibbons.

DIVISION 14.

KELLY & Co., Messrs.—*Organ Harpsichord* or *Claviorganum*, by Crang. 1745.

Case XXVII.

ELKINGTON & Co., Messrs.—Reproductions in Electrotype, of Horns, etc.
—— Vase de l'Helicon en argent et fer repoussé, by Morel Ladeuil.

Case XXVIII.

CORRER, Count GIOVANNI.—Four *Pastoral Horns*, in wood, of remote date.
—— *Viola da Spalta* (7 stringed). No maker's name or date.
—— *Viola da Spalta*, by Pietro Zenatto, of Treviso. 1683–4.
—— *Flûte traversière*, Cyprus wood.
—— Three *Flauti traversie.*
—— Two *Viole da Gamba.*

Wall Case.

PAGDEN, Mrs., and Miss FERRARI.—*Bible Regal*, a rare keyboard reed instrument (so called because it closes like a book). English. 16th century.

CHAPPELL & Co., Messrs.—*Double Spinet*, by Hans Ruckers the Elder. About 1590, Antwerp.
—— Autograph letter from Beethoven to Ferdinand Ries.

MUSEUM AND PUBLIC LIBRARY, MAIDSTONE.—*Clavichord*, gebunden and with the two lowest sharps divided. Dated 1726. Said to have belonged to Handel, and to have been used by him for composing on journeys.

KUNST UND GEWERBE MUSEUM, BERLIN.—*Clavecin Brisé* or *Reise Spinet*, by Marius. Said to have belonged to Frederick the Great.

BOURNE, Mr. TEMPLE.—*Virginal*, English, by Jacobus White. 1656.

CHAPPELL & Co., Messrs.—*Virginal*, by Leversedge. 1666, London. Painted with views of St. James's Park, &c. Said to have belonged to Nell Gwynne.

———

HILTON, The Rev. L. K.—*Spinet*, English, by C. Haward. Second half 17th century.

PICTURE.

OXFORD, UNIVERSITY OF.—98. Portrait of William Gregory.

DIVISION 15.

Case XXIX.

SAMARY, Mons. GEORGES.—*Cetera*, Italian. 16th century. Labelled "Antonius Olinone Plebanus Podis Lastne anno 1536, fecit."
—— *Head of a Violoncello*, carved and varnished, French. 18th century.
—— *Head of a Bass Viol*, carved with a woman's head, French. 17th century.
—— *Cetera*, Italian, by Gaspar da Salo, of Brescia. 16th century.
—— *Head of Bass Viol*, carved with Fool's Head, French. End of 16th century.
—— *Violé d'Amour*, by Paul Alletsee. Munich, 1726.
—— *Pochette*, Louis XIII., by Matthias Hoffman. Antwerp.
—— *Pochette and Bow*, French, by Antonius Médaro. Nancy, 1666.
—— *Cistre*, French, by Gérard De la Blanque. Lille, 1777.

MALCOLM, Mr. ALEXANDER, Venice.—*Hunting Horn*, carved ivory, German. 18th century.

Case XXX.

VALDRIGHI, Mons. le.Comte.—*Violin*.
—— *Violin*, rich purfling.
——— "
——— *Cetera*, Italian, carved with woman's head, and mermaid under the finger-board.
—— *Violin*.
—— *Viol*.
—— *Viola d'Amore*.
—— *Zither*.
—— *Viola*.
—— *Iron Harmonicon*.

Case XXXI.

SCHEUBLEER, Mons. D. F.—*Marahha*. Instrument used in Surinam.

SCHEURLEER, Mons. D. F.—*Violin* (child's), by Job. Cuypers.
About 1790.

—— *Shophar*. Jewish instrument, with inscription.

—— *Flageolet*. 17th century. Probably Dutch.

—— *Pochette*. Probably Dutch.

—— *Flúte d'Amour*. Signed Van Heerde.

—— *Pochette*, by Johannes F. Cuypers. 1783.

—— *Wiero*. Instrument used in Surinam.

—— *Cither*. Johannes Cuypers, fecit 1792.

—— *Violin*, by Johannes Swarts. 1634.

—— „ by J. Bomomentin. 1689.

—— „ „ „ 1683.

—— „ by Pieter Rombouts. 1712.

—— „

—— „ *and bow.*

Wall Case.

WINDSOR, The TRUSTEES of the late Mr. H. BENYON.—*Double
Bass*, English, by William Forster. Made for H.M.
George III.

—— *Double Bass*, Italian, by Francesco Ruggerius, of Cremona. Date 1679.

ROTHSCHILD, Baron FERDINAND . DE.—*Upright Piano*, by
Broadwood, with stool and music case. The case is
made by Wright and Mansfield from a Square Piano of
1799. With paintings commemorating the battle of the
Nile.

SAMARY, Mons. GEORGES.—*Chitarrone,* or Roman *Lute*. Labelled " Magno dieffoprüchar à Venetia." 1608, Italian.

DE SELVIER, Mr. E.—*Cottage Pianoforte*. Said to have
belonged to Lady Morgan. Louis XVI. Case.

BROADWOOD & SONS, Messrs. JOHN.—*Model* of the action of
the above.

MATTHEWS, Mr. J. W.—*Contra-Bass*, Italian, by Nicholas
Amati. 1678.

.—*Double Bass.*

.—*Violone.*

DECCA, Mdlle. MARIE.—*Cistre*, French. 18th century.

JENKIN, Mr. J. C.—*Chitarrone.*

.—*Gender.*

WYBARD, Mr. H. J.—*Dital Harp.*

OAKELEY, Sir HERBERT.—*Hurdy Gurdy,* ancient.

EXETER, Marquess of.—*Dital Harp.*

CHESTER, Mr. JOHN.—*Gender.*

KENNEDY, Mr. E. H.—*Chitarrone.* 1760.

ANDERSON's COLLEGE, GLASGOW—*Guitar.*

SAMARY, Mons. GEORGES.—*Cavalry Trumpet and Banner.*
Nuremburg, 18th century.

   .—Violoncello.

———

GILBEY, Mr. WALTER.—*Upright Square Piano,* by William
Southwell, of Dublin. Paintings by Angelica Kauff-
mann. 1798.

PICTURE.

OXFORD, UNIVERSITY OF.—99. Portrait of Christopher
Simpson.

DIVISION 16.

Case **XXXII.**

MAHILLON, Mons. VICTOR.—Reproductions.
—— *Cromorne.*
—— *Sordino.*
—— ,,
—— ,,
—— ,,
—— *Fagotto,* in ivory.
—— *Bass,* Musette in C.
—— *Zincke,* in F.
—— ,, ,, G.
—— ,, ,, G.
—— ,, ,, C.
—— ,, with Mute.
—— *Bassoon.* Beginning of 17th century.
—— *Flûte traversière* in C.
—— ,, ,, ,, F.
—— ,, ,, ,, E.
—— ,, ,, ,, D.

Case **XXXIII.**

CONSERVATOIRE ROYAL OF BRUSSELS.—*Basset Horn,* with
    upright bell.
—— *Oboe,* two keys. 18th century.
—— *Schalmey,* German.
—— *Oboe d'Amour,* by J. H. Rottenburgh, of Brussels.
—— *Large Oboe,* one key, German.
—— *Oboe da Caccia.*
—— *Musette,* German.
—— *Oboe,* with two different pieces for changing the pitch,
    by Lempp, of Vienna.
—— *Oboe* (Three Keyed), by Rottenburgh.
—— *Zincke,* or *Cornet à boquin,* in C.
—— *Clarinet,* in B flat, Five Keys, by N. M. Raingo, of
    Mons.
—— *Clarinet,* two keys, by G. A. Rottenburgh, of Brussels.
—— ,, *d'Amour.* Signed " P. Piena à Milan."

CONSERVATOIRE ROYAL OF BRUSSELS.—Part of a *Basset Horn*, Italian.
—— Two *Clarinets*, three keys, by Denner (the inventor).
—— „ by J. B. Willems.
—— *Flute* in form of a column with capital and base. In key of G.
—— *Fagottino.* Signed Sherer.
—— *Tibia*, Greco-Roman. Copy of one of four found at Pompeii. Original in the Museum at Naples.
—— *Flageolet*, ivory.
—— „
—— „
—— *Zincke* or *Tenor Cornet à boquin* in C.
—— *Provençal Galoubet*, with three holes.
—— *Flauto Dolce.*
—— „ one key.
—— *Flûte à bec.*
—— *Flauto Dolce*, carved boxwood. Signed T. T. Coppens.
—— *Harmonic Flute*, with double column of air, tuned in thirds.
—— *Bass Flûte traversière*, by T. Lot.
—— Part of *Flute.* Copy of instrument found in Pompeii.

Case XXXIV.

CONSERVATOIRE ROYAL OF BRUSSELS. *Pochette (Kit), Bow and Case.* Paris, 1667.
—— *Bronze Whistle*, ancient Roman.
—— Set of *Cromornes* in case. 16th century. The only complete set known to exist.
—— *Musette*, French.

Wall Case.

LEYLAND, Mr. F. R.—*Harpsichord*, by Hans Ruckers the Younger. 1642. Decorated case with paintings inside the top.

RESSE, Count.—*Serpentaccio.*

KLINCKERFUSS, Mons. B.—*Fortepiano*, in spinet-shaped case.

CORRER, Count GIOVANNI.—*Chitarra turca.* 16th century.

DE LISLE, Lord.—*Clavicembalo (Harpsichord.)* The instrument removed from the outer case.

Formerly the property of Queen Christina of Sweden, her crest being carved on each side of the keyboard. The outer case and stand in *gesso duro*, with two portraits of Queen Christina, are by Giovanni Lorenzo Bernini, who died in 1680.

CORRER, Count GIOVANNI.—*Viola da Spalta*, by Pietro Zenatto of Treviso. 1683–4.

—— *Viola da Gamba*, by Giglio (figlio) Siciliano, of Venice. 1670.

—— *Cither*, Turkish. 1800.

———

ALLEN, Mr. E. H.—Bust of J. B. Viotti.

PICTURE.

OXFORD, UNIVERSITY OF.—100. Portrait of Colonel Blathwayt.

DIVISION 17.

Case XXXV.

GRAHAM, the late Mr. W.—*Grand Piano*, made by Messrs. John Broadwood & Sons. 1880. The case painted in medallions with the story of Orpheus. Outside the top a Poet and a Muse. Inside the top an allegorical painting of the Earth with her good and bad children. By Mr. Edward Burne Jones, A.R.A.

Case XXXVI.

VINTER, Mr. H. S.—*Metronome*, by James Condliffe, of Liverpool. Late 18th century.

NIBBS, Mr. RICHARD H.—*Metronome*, by Pridgen, of York.

MEYERS, Mr. S. H.—*Metronome*. One of the earliest made by Maelzel.

AMELS, Herr JEAN.—Scheibler's own *Tonometer* of 56 *Tuning Forks*, for precisely determining pitch. Described in Mr. A. J. Ellis's lecture on the History of Musical Pitch.

.—*Ivory Flute.*

LIGGINS, Mr. H.—*Flute*, silver keys.

FIELDING, Major-General the Hon. PERCY, C.B.—*Bulgarian Shepherd's Pipe.*

GLEN, Messrs. J. & R.—*Double Flageolet.*

CHRIST CHURCH, OXFORD.—Two *Old English Hoboys or Waits.* (Zincken.)

VALDRIGHI, Count L. F. — *Cor Anglais*, by Fornari, of Venice.

CLARKE, Colonel TREVOR.—*Ivory Bass Flute.* 18th century.

.—*Cor Anglais.*

E

KLINCKERFUSS, Herr.—*Double Harpischord*, by Ring, decorated.

Wall Case.

GOLD^SMID, Sir JULIAN.—*Guitar* of Domenico Tallas. Venice, 1600.
—— *Guitar*, by Sella, Venetian. 1638.
—— „ by Joachim Tielke. Hamburg, 1670.
—— „ ten-stringed, Portuguese. 16th century.
—— „ Italian, sound-board inlaid with ivory and mother of pearl.
—— „
—— *Keyed Cither.*

JOSEPH, Mr. EDWARD.—*Keyed Harp Lute.*
—— *Violin*, shoe-shaped.
—— *Chitarrone.*
—— *Lute.* 16th century.
—— *Clock*, Louis XVI., gilt bronze mounting, and old Dresden figures of a monkey band.
—— *Cetera*, Italian.

DALE, Mr. W.—*Spinet*, by Thomas Haxby. 1764, York.

DUNCAN, Mr. G. CUTHBERTSON.—Bust of Nicolo Paganini.

PICTURES.

HOPKINSON, Messrs. J. & J.—101. Portrait of Domenici Dragonetti.

OXFORD, UNIVERSITY OF.—102. Portrait of Matthew Lock.

STREET, Mr. J. E.—103. Portraits of Dr. Maurice Green and Dr. Hoadly, by Hayman.

LAWRENCE, Mrs. E.—104. Tartini, by F. Smallfield.

BROWN, Mr. J. J.—105. *The Troubadour*, by Harman Philips.

HOPKINSON, Messrs. J. & J.—106. Portrait of Robert Lindley.

BARNARD, Mr. T. T.—107. Portrait of Haydn, by Sir M. Shee, P.R.A. 1796.

OXFORD, UNIVERSITY OF.—108. Portrait of Father Bernhard Smith.
—— 109. Portrait of Nicholas Lanière.

DIVISION 18.

Case XXXVII.

AMSTERDAM, MUNICIPALITY OF.—Two *Schalmeyen*, German 2nd half of 17th century.
—— Three *Schalmeyen*, German. 1st half of 17th century.
—— *Trumpet*, French, by Colbert, Rheims.
—— Part of a *Trumpet*, German. Early 16th century.

HARPER, Mr. THOMAS.—*Trumpet*, silver mounted, English, by William Bull. About 1680.
—— *Trumpet*, English, by John Harris. About 1730.

WEBB, Mr. JOSEPH.—*Trumpet*, English. 1814.
Carried by Sergeant-Major Webb, of the 5th Dragoon Guards, Field Trumpeter to the Duke of Wellington. Sounded the grand charge at the battle of Salamanca.

MALCOLMSON, Mr. A. W.—*Cavalry Trumpet*, embossed, very heavy mouthpiece, English, by William Sandbach. 18th century.

    .—*Trombone*.

EXETER, The Marquess of.—Two *Hunting Horns*, English. 18th century.

HARTSHORNE, Lieut.-Col.—*Fog Horn*, Cornish. About 1700. Marked " J. O." (John Oliver).

OAKELEY, Sir HERBERT.—Stucco Cast of Peruvian *Syrinx*.
—— *Bâton*, silver mounted.
—— *Flageolet*, Ebony.
—— *Double Flageolet*.

STEWART, Sir ROBERT.— *Presentation Bâton*, silver-gilt, chased and set with precious stones. 1848.

WILMOTT, Miss E. A.—Two *Walking Stick Flutes*.
—— *Double Flute*.
—— *Mukhavinai*, Hindustan.
—— *Ivory Octave Flute*.
—— *Octave Flute*.

WILMOTT, Miss E A.—*Cor Anglais.*
—— *Mukhavinai,* Hindustani instrument.

BOERS, Mons. T. C.—*Korthourt.*

Case XXXVIII.

KLINCKERFUSS, Herr B.—*Oboe de Caccia.*
—— *Flageolet.*

ALLEN, Mr. E. HERON.—*Flageolet,* Pyrancean.

CLARKE, Colonel TREVOR.—*Musette* or *Hautbois.* Modern.

FITZHENRY, Mr. J. H.—*Fife.*

GLEN, Messrs. J. & R.—*English Horn* or *Cor Anglais,* by
Cramer & Co.
—— *Flageolet.*
—— *Small Bassoon.*
—— *Cor Anglais.*
—— *Flute.*

VALDRIGHI, COUNT L. F.—*Flautone,* wood and brass,
Italian. Early 17th century.
—— *Cor Anglais,* wood, by Mazzaroni, of Bologna. 18th
century.
—— Two *Fifes,* ivory, 17th century, Italian. Used by the
fifers of the Dukes of Modena.

PARKER, Mr. ROBERT.—*Double Flageolet,* by Bainbridge.

FINCH, Colonel WYNNE.—*Pibgorn* or *Welsh Horn,* from the
Isle of Anglesea. About 1700.

MYERS, Mr. V. M.—" *Shouphar* " or *Ramshorn,* used by the
Jews in places of worship.

LIDDLE, Mr. R. K.—*Oboe,* by T. Collier, boxwood, with two
silver keys. London, 1775.

WILSON, Mr. ROBERT.—The *Emmelian* or *Trio Flageolet,* by
W. Bainbridge. 1830.

SUFFOLK, Mr. E.—*Bass Flute.*

KEENE, Mr. CHARLES.—*Stockhorn* (Lowland shepherd's
pipe).

Wall Case.

BROADWOOD & SONS, Messrs. JOHN—*Spinet,* by Thomas
Hitchcock, London.

BOX, Mr. JAMES.—*Nail Violin*, on stand. About 17th century.

TAPHOUSE, Mr. T. W.—*Spinet*, by Joseph Baudin. 1723. London. Belonged to Simon Fraser (Lord Lovat), and Dr. Rimbault.

CORRER, Count GIOVANNI.—Two *Trombe Marine*. 14th century.

KENNEDY, Mr. E. H.—*Serpent*, English. 1680.

SAMARY, Mons. GEORGES.—Two *Cavalry Trumpets*, painted with serpent's head. End of 18th century.

NEWMAN, Mr. A. B. A.—*Horn*, Nuremburg. 18th century.
—— *Trumpet*.
—— *Tenor Trombone*.

.—*Serpent*.

RESSE, Count PIO.—*Serpent*, black wood, engraved, Italian. Early 17th century.

ANGRAVE, Mr. CHARLES.—*Singing Trumpet*. Date unknown. Used in the Parish Church of East Leake, Nottinghamshire, during Divine Service, up to about 1840.

————

McINTYRE, Mr. C. N.—Book of the Club of True High landers (two vols.). A record of the Dress, Arms, Customs, Arts and Science of the Highlanders.

CROSTHWAITE, Mr.—*Rock Harmonicon* or *Musical Stones*.

Copy of the original label, in Crosthwaite's Museum, Keswick, in the year 1786:—

" Here lie 16 Stones reduced to Music by the Author of this Museum, who found them in the bed of Greta river from 12 to 18 furlongs East of Keswick. More than 200 gentry have declared them to be the first set of music stones that ever was in the World, and one of the greatest curiosities in England. They are very hard, strike fire with steel Their country name is Skiddaw Whintin and the Mineralogists call them Gneiss. They are an original stone, no petrifaction being ever found in them. Found the first 6 Music Stones on the 11th of June, 1785."

—— *Small Barrel Organ*, by Joseph Beloudy.

PICTURES.

OXFORD, UNIVERSITY OF.—110. Portrait of Orlando Lassus.

.—111. Harpsichord Top. Flowers painted on the inside.

LUSHINGTON, Mr. VERNON.—112. Oil Painting, Italian. Musicians and Huntsmen. 16th century.

McINTYRE, Mr. C. N.—113. Sketches of Musical Instruments.

OXFORD, UNIVERSITY OF.—114. Portrait of John Hilton.

DIVISION 19.

Case XXXIX.

RUDALL, CARTE & Co., Messrs.—*Tenor Clarinet*, by Key.
1820–1830.
—— *Double Flageolet*, by Bainbridge, London. Patent,
1819.
—— *Triple Flageolet*, by Bainbridge, London.
—— *Oboe*, by Cahusac.
—— „ by Power, London. Late 18th century.
—— *Clarinet*, by T. Key. 1810–1820.
—— „ by Cramer, London. 1770–1790.
—— „ „ „ „
—— „ „ „ „
—— *Bass Flute*, by MacGregor, London. Patent, 1810.

TAMPLINI, Signor G.—*Contra Fagotto* (Double Bassoon), by
Marzoli and Triebert. (*On top of Case.*)
—— *Bassoon*, by Ward, London. Patent, 1853.
—— *Tenoroon* (Tenor Bassoon), by Marzoli, Paris. 1850.
—— *Bassoon*, by Ward, London. Patent 1853.

KOHLER & SON, Messrs.—*Clarinet*, 13 keys. James Wood,
London. Patents, 1800, 1814 and 1819.

RUDALL, CARTE & Co.—*Fagottino*.
—— *Bassoon*, 4 keys. Without name and date.
—— „ 8 keys. Cramer & Key. Before 1802.
—— *Flûte-à-bec* (English flute). 18th century.
—— *Fife*, by Key.
—— *German Flute*, by Willis.
—— *Flute*, by Wafford.
—— „ „ Potter, London. 1805.
—— *English Flute*, by Bainbridge. 1810.
—— *Flute*, by Monzani. 1815.
—— „ ebony, by Drouet.
—— „ boxwood, by Rudall & Rose. 1820–25.
—— *Tenor Flute*, by R. Burleigh. About 1855.
—— *Bass Flute*, by R. Burleigh. About 1855.

RUDALL, CARTE & Co.—*Flute*, by Koch, of Vienna. About
1830. The late Professor Sedlatzeck's flute.
—— *Conical Flute*, Boehm's system of fingering. Between
1840 and 1848.
—— *Flute*, by Ward, London. Patent, 1842.
—— *Flûte d'Amour*, by Ward, London. Patent, 1842.

BEVIGNANI, Chevalier.—*Flute*, ivory, by Monzani. 1812–
1820.
—— *Flute*, ivory, by Monzani. 1820–1824.
—— *Flûte d'Amour*. by Monzani. 1810–1820.

YEATMAN, Mr. M.—*Flute*, glass. About 1830.

BARRETT, Mr. W. L.—*Flute*, ivory, by Clementi. About 1823.
—— *Flute*. cocoa-wood, by Clementi. About 1827.
—— „ box-wood, by Paine & Hopkins. About 1825.

HAYS, Mr. A.—*Flute*, 11 keys, Toulou, Paris. About 1835.
—— *Cylinder Flute*, by T. Boehm, Munich. About 1851.

WELCH, Mr. C.—*Flute*, by Siccama, London. Patent, 1848.

Case XL.

STEUART, Mr. C. DURRANT, of Dalguise, N.B.—*Harp*,
known as Queen Mary's Harp, and given by that
Queen to Beatrix Gardyne of Banchory.
—— *Harp*, known as the Lamont Harp, brought into the
family of Robertson of Lude, about 1460.

SPENCER, Earl.—*Hunting Horn*, ivory, Indo-Portuguese.
Early 16th century, with the Arms and Badges of
Ferdinand and Isabella.

Case XLI.

SKENE, Miss. — *Bagpipes*, red velvet embroidered, with
separate bellows.

They belonged to Prince Charles Edward Stuart, and were bequeathed by
him to one of his attendants, from whose family they were purchased in Rome
in the year 1802 by the late James Skene, of Rubislaw.

—— Bellows of Northumbrian Pipes.
—— *Ancient Chanter*.
—— *Calabrian Bagpipes*, Italian. 18th century.
—— Small *Irish Bagpipes*.

GLEN, Messrs. J. & R.—*Lowland Bagpipes*.
—— *Highland Bagpipes*, Scotch, carved with Celtic design.
1409.
—— *Irish Bagpipes*.

FAIRLESS, Dr. W. D.—*Northumbrian Small Pipes.* About 1840.

GLEN, Messrs. J. & R.—*Musette.*
—— *Cornemuse.*

Case XLII.

DOVER, CORPORATION OF.—*Trumpet*, Bronze. "De a Lemaine me fecit." 13th century.

The Corporation of Dover were in ancient times assembled by order of the Mayor by blowing of the horn. The minutes of their proceedings commenced with the words, "At a common horn blowing." The horn blowing continued down to 1670. The horn is still used by the Corporation for certain ceremonies.

GREEN, Mr. FRED. J.—*Music Box* and *Work Box* in the shape of a Grand Piano, French. Late 18th century, or early 19th.

SAMARY, Mons. GEORGES.—*Pair of Candlesticks*, in the form of trumpets, silver, French, Louis XVI.

JACKSON, The Rev. J. C.—*Violin Delft.* 18th century.
—— *Tuning Forks.* 18th century.

DAVY Mr. G. B.—Beethoven's *Watch.*
—— *Mask* of Beethoven, taken about four years before his death, and piece of his hair.

MACKESON, Mr. H. B.—*Seal* of the Corporation of Hythe, showing a similar Trumpet to the one in this case.

CANTERBURY, CORPORATION OF.—*Burgmote Horn.*

RAVENNA, MUNICIPALITY OF.—Bacchetta del Maestro Concertatore Cav° Angelo Mariani.

MACKESON, Mr. H. B.—*Ship's Trumpet*, in two parts, each three feet in length, English. 14th century. (See also the seal.)

JOSEPH, Mr. EDWARD.—*Gold Enamel Harp.*

SMART, Miss.—*Cast* of Weber's Hand. Taken immediately after his death, 5th of June, 1826.

MATTHEW, Mr. J. W.—Portrait of Beethoven, by Letronne. Given to Charles Neate during his stay in Vienna in the year 1815.

MOSCHELES, Mr. F.—*Cast*, Mendelssohn's Hand. *Music Desk*, decorated by Mendelssohn.

STONYHURST, The Very REV. the RECTOR OF.—*Handbell*, inscribed "Me fecit Johannes a fine a." 1548.
—— *Handbell*, Russian.

MAITLAND, Mr. J. A. FULLER.—*Sanctus Bell*, Swiss. 18th century.

STEWART, Sir ROBERT.—*Model of the first Concertina*, invented by Wheatstone.
—— Haydn's *Breast Pin*.

WEALE, Mr. W. H. JAMES.—Medal Portrait of Michael Mercator, of Venloo, Maker of Virginals to Floris d'Egmont, Cardinal Wolsey, and Henry VIII. 1491–1544.

THEWALT, Mons.—Two *Child's Rattles*, silver, German. End of 17th century.
—— *Mug*, Stoneware, with musical subjects, Siegburg ware. About 1500.
—— *Clock*, Brass, Gilt, and engraved with musical subjects, French. 17th century.

JOSEPH, Mr. EDWARD.—*Patch Box* in the form of a brass fiddle.
—— *Bonbonnière* or Patch Box, Battersea enamel.

HILL, Miss ALICE.—Miniature *Guitar* and *Mandoline* made of tortoiseshell, inlaid with pearl, &c., modern Italian work.

.—*Delft Violin.*

Wall Case.

HOPKINSON, Lieut.-General H., C.S.I.—*Double Clavecin*, or *Harpsichord*, by André Ruckers. 1614, Antwerp. Painting inside the top attributed to Van der Meulen.

HIPKINS, Mr. A. J.—Drawing of Soundboard of the above, barring and decoration, by R. Maitland.

H.R.H. THE PRINCE OF WALES.—*Cavalry Bugle.*
This bugle, carried by Trumpeter Smith, sounded the charge at the moonlight charge of the Household Cavalry at Kassassin.

STONE, Dr. W. H.—Pair of *Oboi da Caccia or Alti Fagotti*, by Savary.

YORKSHIRE PHILOSOPHICAL SOCIETY.—*Virginal.* "Thomas White, 1651."

WARRINGTON, CORPORATION OF.—*Virginal.*

.—Front board of a harpsichord, painted by

HENRY, Mr. J. SNOWDEN.—*Chamber Organ*, Flemish? 1592."

The inscriptions are E. Hoffheimer, fec. 1592, and (in Flemish) " Praise the Lord with a loud tune on the organ. Psalm 150, A.D. 1592." The stops are stopped diapason, flute and vox humana. All the pipes are of wood, and, with the exception of two or three, are elaborately carved.

TAPHOUSE, Mr. T. W.—*Serpent*, English. About 1740.

OAKELEY, Sir HERBERT.—*Serpent* Copper, with four keys and six holes.

VALDRIGHI, Count L. F.—*Lid of Spinet*, Italian. 17th century.

———

BROADWOOD & SONS, Messrs.—*Pianoforte* in shape of a Spinet, by Crang Hancock. 1782, London.

PICTURES, &C.

PLEYEL, WOLFF & Co., Paris.—115. Three Frames containing Autograph Letters, &c., of I. Pleyel, C. Pleyel, Montivault, Kalkbrenner, Cherubini, Schumann, Chopin, G. Sand, Mendelssohn, Sir Robert Peel, Thomas, David, Auber, Gounod, Weber, Meyerbeer, Cramer, Halévy, and Rossini.

OXFORD, UNIVERSITY OF.—116. Portrait of J. P. Eiffert.

DIVISION 20.

On Screen B.

DUNCAN, Mr. G. CUTHBERTSON.—*Paganini, Nicolo.* Quartet (No. 11), in B major, for violin, viola, guitar, and violincello. Unpublished.

—— *Paganini, Nicolo.* Quartet (No. 15), in A major, for violin, viola, guitar, and violoncello. Unpublished.

—— *Paganini, Nicolo.* Quartet (No. 13), in F. major, for violin, viola, guitar, and violoncello. Unpublished.

—— *Paganini, Nicolo.* Quartet (No. 14), in A major, for violin, viola, guitar, and violoncello. Unpublished.

—— *Paganini, Nicolo.* Quartet (No. 12), in A minor, for violin, viola, guitar, and violoncello. Unpublished.

—— *Paganini, Nicolo.* Eleven autograph letters, addressed to L. G. Germi. Various dates.

—— *Paganini, Nicolo.* Portrait (? unique), engraved by A. Gravagni, after G. Bignami.

—— *Paganini, Nicolo.* Autograph MS. An account of some of his instruments.

—— *Paganini, Nicolo.* Quartet (No. 10), in A major, for violin, viola, guitar, and violoncello. Unpublished.

—— *Paganini, Nicolo.* Autograph music

ORLANDINI, Madame M. MORIANI.—Seven autograph letters from Gaetano Donizetti to N. Moriani, various dates, Donizetti, Gaetano. Fragment of MS. of " Il Bravo."

—— Four lines of poetry by Gaetano Donizetti. Autograph.

MOSCHELES, Mr. FELIX.—*Cherubini, Luigi.* Canon, composed in 1811.

—— *Clementi, Muzio.* Study, dated March, 18—.

—— *Praeger, Emil.* Pen-and-ink drawing, Moscheles' journey from London to Leipzig. 1846.

—— *Döhler Theodore.* Study, autograph.

—— *Moscheles, Ignaz.* Study, dated March, 1869.

——   „   „   Organ part to Beethoven's 9th symphony.

—— *Mendelssohn Bartholdy, Felix.* Certificate of Doctor's Degree, Leipzig, 1836.

RAVENNA, Municipality of.—MS. of Cavatina "Se mia moglie crepasse una Volta." In Rossini's handwriting, and sung by him at Imola, 22 April, 1804.
—— *Rossini, G.* Symphony in D minor, written when a boy at the Conventello of Mezzano, Ravenna.

PADDISON, Mrs.—*Spohr, L.* Fragments of MS. of "Calvary."

ROCHE, Miss CHARLOTTE.—*Weber, Carl Maria Von.* MS. scena from "Oberon," 1826.
—— *Thalberg, Sigismund.* Study, autograph.

TAPHOUSE, Mr. T. W.—*Czerny, Charles.* Souvenir Theatral.
—— *Cramer, J. B.* Andantino, composed in London, 20 October, 1844.

DUNCAN G. CUTHBERTSON.—*Paganini, Nicolo.* Autograph sonata for violin and viola.
—— *Paganini, Nicolo.* Autograph music for violin.

LUCCA, SIGNOR FRANCESCO. Mercadante, Motet "O Phillippe spes salutis," for chorus and organ. Dated 1836.
—— *Rossini, G.* Recitative "Un vero Militar" and Aria "Alla Gloria un genio." Full score.
—— *Mercadante.* Motet for tenor solo, chorus, and orchestra. Orchestral score only.
—— *Donizetti, Gaetano.* Canzone Napoletana.

ORLANDINI, Madame M. MORIANI.—*Tamburini, A.* Autograph letter to N. Moriani. Paris, 26 October, 1839.
—— *Morlacchi, F.* "Ave Maria," dated 15th August, 1841. Full score.
—— *Reissiger, C. G.* MS. Offertory "Laetamini in Deo." For soprano, tenor, chorus and orchestra. Full score. Dated 27 July, 1843.
—— *Verdi, Giuseppe.* Romanza "Oh Dolore," from "Attila." Full score.
—— *Verdi, Giuseppe.* Autograph letter to N. Moriani.
—— *Mario.* Autograph letter to N. Moriani.
—— *Schubert, Franz.* Autograph letter to L. Schneider.
—— *Meyerbeer, G.* Autograph letter to Schönlein.
—— *Bellini, Vincenzo.* Scena "Se Meditata e pronta" and Aria "La Speranza ond'is son lieto." Full score.
—— *Ricca Federigo.* Introduction to Act II. of "Rolla." Full score.
—— *Bellini, Vincenzo.* Autograph letter to N. Moriani. Dated 3 April, 1841.

ORLANDINI, Madame M. MORIANA.—*Ricci Luigi*. Autograph letter to N. Moriani. Dated Trieste, 21 December, 1855.
—— *Rossini, G.* Autograph letter to Prince Trubeckoy.
—— *Proch, Heinrich.* Autograph letter to N. Moriani.
—— *Panseron, A.* Autograph letter. Dated Paris, 14 October, 1815.
—— *Rossini, G.* Autograph letter to Coun^t M. Wielhorski.
—— *Campana, Fabio.* Autograph letter. Dated Leghorn, 25 March, 1842.
—— Scena and cavature from an opera. Full score.

HUEFFER, Mr. FRANCIS.—*Schumann, Robert.* Autograph letter to R. W. Von Zuccalmaglio. Dated Leipsig, 23 April, 1839.
—— *Franz. Robert.* Autograph letter to Francis Hueffer. Dated Halle, 5 November, 1883, enclosing a fragment of a song, "Er ist gekommen."

Case XLIV.

HER MAJESTY THE QUEEN.—*Grand Pianoforte*, by S. & P. Erard, of London. The paintings in Vernis Martin, from a harpsichord which belonged to Anne of Austria.
—— Two *Silver Kettledrums*, with bannerets, from St. James' Palace.

On Screen C.

MARSHALL, Mr. JULIAN.—Portrait of Farinelli, by Wagner, after Amiconi.
—— Portrait of Beethoven, by Müller, after Decker.
—— House in which Beethoven was born.
—— Caricature Portrait of Beethoven.
—— Original Manuscript, by Beethoven.
—— Portrait of Beethoven taken after death.
—— Portraits of Cherubini.
—— Autograph letter of Cherubini.
—— Original MS. by Cherubini.
—— Portrait of Weber (Composer), by Lane, after Cawse.
—— Autograph note of Weber.
—— Original MS. by Weber, "O Araby, dear Araby."
—— Autograph letter of Weber to Charles Kemble. 1825.
—— Portrait of Dr. Blow, by R. White.
—— Receipt given by Dr. Blow (£483 6s. 8d.) for the King's Musicians, March 22, 1686.
—— Portrait of Clerambault. Organist.

MARSHALL, Mr. JULLIAN.—Portrait of Farinelli, with Allegorical Figures, by Wagner, after Amiconi.
—— Portrait of Berton, by Saint Aubin, after Dumont.
—— „ Chopin.
—— Autograph Letter of Chopin.
—— Original Manuscript, by Berton.
—— Portraits of Clementi (drawings).
—— Original Manuscript, by Clementi.
—— Portrait of Cramer, by Thomson, after Barber.
—— „ Erard.
—— Original Manuscript, by Cramer. Variations to "Rule Britannia."
—— Portraits of Auber.
—— Original MS. by Auber.
—— Autograph letter of Auber, 1842.
—— Original Manuscript, by Méhul.
—— Portrait of Wagner, drawing by Holiday. 1877.
—— Portrait of Wagner when middle-aged.
—— Portrait of Wagner when young.
—— Wagner conducting at the Albert Hall. Sketches by Holiday.
—— Portrait of Hummel. Drawing by Hayter.
—— „ Gluck (drawing).
—— Original Manuscript, by Gluck (Air de danse dans Admète).
—— Portrait of Gluck, by St. Aubin.
—— Autograph Letter of Farinelli, April, 1756.
—— Portrait of De Bariot. Caricature by Danton.
—— Portrait of Baillot (Composer).
—— Original Manuscript, by Baillot, composed for his friend Cherubini.
—— Portrait of Méhul (Composer), by Quenedey. 1808.
—— „ Martini (Composer), by Adam, after Kreützinger.
—— "Il Ris," by Martini. Signed by the Composer.

Wall Cases.

HER MAJESTY THE QUEEN.—*Double Harpsichord*, by Shudi. No. 94. 1740.
—— *Basso di Camera.* Bequeathed to H.R.H. The Prince Consort by Signor Dragonetti.
—— *Double Harpsichord*, by Hans Ruckers. 1612.

From Windsor Castle. The "large harpsichord" named in Handel's will may have been this instrument. The keyboards are new.

—— Ten *Silver Trumpets*, with bannerets, from St. James's Palace.

PICTURES, &c.

PLEYEL, WOLFF & Co.—117. Three Frames containing Autograph Letters, &c., of Boccherini, Haydn, Bach, Herold, Berlioz, Spontini, Halévy, Beethoven, F. Ries, and Mozart.

OXFORD, UNIVERSITY OF.—118. Portrait of Dr. Croft.

DIVISION 21.

On Screen D.

MARSHALL, Mr. JULIAN.—Portrait of Braham, drawn by Deighton, 1830, and autograph letters of Braham.
—— Original manuscript and letters by Dr. Burney.
—— Portraits of Dragonetti.
—— Portrait of Bennett.
—— „ Paganini.
—— „ „ playing at a concert.
—— Autograph letter and original manuscript by Paganini.
—— Portrait of Dragonetti, by Bartolozzi.
—— Autograph letter and original MS. of Dragonetti.
—— Portrait of Madame Malibran de Beriot, by Sharp.
—— Autograph Letters of Madame Malibran de Beriot (naming her terms).
—— Handbook for 'Elijah,' by Mendelssohn. First performance. 1847. Signed.
—— Portrait of Mendelssohn, by Reyher. 1872.
—— „ Charles Dibdin, by J. Young, after T. Phillips.
—— Autograph letter and original manuscript of Dibdin's.
—— Original manuscript by Mendelssohn, "I would that my Love."
—— Original manuscript by Mendelssohn, 'I would that my Love. 1844.
—— Autograph letters of Mendelssohn. 1837 and 1847.
—— Portrait of Mozart at the age of seven.
—— „ Mozart, by Quenedey.
—— Original manuscript by Mozart, 'Fantasia, in C minor, for the Piano.' 1865.
—— Original manuscript by Mozart, 'Sonata for the Piano.' 1784.
—— Portrait of Dr. Pepusch, from a Painting at Oxford.
—— „ Gamble (Composer), by Cross.
—— „ Rizio (Rizzio), by Wilkin.
—— „ Viotti (Composer and Violinist). Drawing.
—— Original Manuscript by Viotti. "Duetto for a Violin."
—— Portrait of Bach, by Kütner, after Haussmann.

F

MARSHALL, Mr. JULIAN.—Portrait of C. P. E. Bach.
—— Portrait of Bach's nephew (J. S. Bach), by Griessmann.
—— Original manuscript by C. P. E. Bach.
—— Portrait of Halévy, by Geoffroy, after Zoller.
—— Original manuscript by Halévy.
——   „   „   Herold.
—— Portrait of Herold.

Case XLV.

ST. GALL (Switzerland), Library of.—Graduals and Missals
10th and 17th centuries.
—— Notker Labialis, German translation of the Psalms,
with marginal notes, by Ekkehardt IV. 12th century.
—— Antiphoner and Gradual. 9th century (?), with editions
of the 12th and 13th centuries.

This manuscript is traditionally said to have been copied by Romanus from
S. Gregory, the great Antiphoner at Rome, between 772 and 795, and to have
been brought by him to St. Gall. On one cover are two ivory plaques of the
4th century.

—— Troparium, Gradual and Sequences. 11th century.
Containing Greek Services in Latin characters, .and
Notker Sequences.
—— Troparium. 10th century. Said to contain Notker's
44 melodies to his Sequences.
—— Antiphoner for Vespers. 13th century.

DEKEDONCHEL, Count GEORGES.—Antiphoner Netherlandish.
15th century.

ST. GALL, Switzerland, Library of.—Introits. Written in
1562 by the organist of St. Gall, H. Keller. Illuminated
by Kaspar Härteli of Lindan.

Music is composed by Lupus of Correggio, who, at the request of Abbot
Diethelm, introduced four part singing at St. Gall, in 1531.

FURNIVAL, Dr. F. J.—Facsimiles of " Angelus ad Virginem,"
the Hymne of Chaucer's Clerke of Oxford (Miller's
Tale, A. § 4, 1. 3216) from British 'Museum, Arundel
M.S., 248, folio 154. Circa 1250 to 1260.

LINCOLN, THE DEAN AND CHAPTER OF.—Fragments of a
Treatise on Music. 13th century. English.

SPENCER, EARL.—Fragment of a Book of Sequences. 14th
century.
—— Fragment of an Antiphoner. 12th century.

Case XLVI.

WILLETT, Mr. H.—Volume of Tracts on different subjects. 14th and 15th centuries, with some music of the 16th century. English. The manuscript is open to show "the tune that Alfred played in the Danish camp." (Note on the left margin.)

.—Book of Sequences. 14th century. Flemish.

.—Antiphoner. German. 13th century.

BODLEIAN LIBRARY, OXFORD, Curators of the.—Treatise on Music. 15th century. English.

LINCOLN, Dean and Chapter of.—Fragment of a Treatise on Music. 13th century. English.

ASHBURNHAM, The Earl of.—Treatise on Music. 13th century. With illumination representing King David. 12th century.

BODLEIAN LIBRARY, OXFORD, Curators of the.—Treatise on Music. 14th century. English. The manuscript is opened at folio 59 of the Regulae of Magister Franco, shewing some interesting musical examples.
—— Gradual. 12th century. German.
—— Antiphoner. 11th century. English?
—— Antiphoner. 13th century. English? Bound up with later manuscripts.

ASHBURNHAM, The Earl of.—Fragments of a Gradual, 11th century, and an Antiphoner, 12th century. English.

ROSENTHAL, LUDWIG, Munich.—Antiphoner, according to the Ambrosian Rite. 11th century. North Italian.

CANTERBURY, Dean and Chapter of.—Fragment. 13th century.

CATHOLIC GREGORIAN ASSOCIATION. — Fragment. 15th century.

HUGGINS, Dr. W.—Portion of an Antiphoner and Gradual. 15th century. Southern German.

PETRE, Lord.—Gradual. Early 15th century, with some additional music in a 16th century hand.

COLEMAN, Mr. C. C.—Portions of an Evangelistarium, the music written in finely-formed uncial notes. 15th century. Italian.

MUSIC, Royal College of.—Antiphoner. 1543. French.

SPENCER, Earl.—Pontifical. 15th century.

AMHERST, Mr. W. A. TYSSEN, M.P.—Part of an Antiphoner.
Music written in early neumes. 12th century.

CANTERBURY, The Archbishop of.—Gradual. 14th century.
English.

Case XLVII.

CANTERBURY, The Archbishop of.—Musical Compendium,
by William Chelle. 1526. English.

HERRIES, Lord.—Antiphoner. York use. 15th century.
English.

ASHBURNHAM, The Earl of.—Gradual. 1427.

ROCKSTRO, Mr. W. S.—Choir Book, containing Mass, "Mon
coeur se recommende à vous," by Philippus de Monte.
16th century. German.

BODLEIAN LIBRARY, OXFORD, Curators of the.—Two Anti-
phoners. 15th century. English.
—— Missal. 15th century. Italian.
—— Antiphoner. 15th century. Italian.

CANTERBURY, Dean and Chapter of.—Four leaves of an
Antiphoner. 15th century.

.—Psalter. Netherlandish. 14th century.

ROSENTHAL'S ANTIQUARIAT, MUNICH.—Hymnal of the Greek
Church. Circa. 1550.

CATHOLIC GREGORIAN ASSOCIATION, ABBÉ BONHOMME.—
Copies of musical notation from manuscripts in the
chief libraries of Europe.

Case XLVIII.

ST. JOHN'S COLLEGE, CAMBRIDGE, The Master and Fellows
of. — Masses by Dr. Fayrfax, John Taverner, &c.,
English. Temp. Henry VIII.
—— Sarum Processional. English. 14th century.
—— Processional, English. 14th century. Formerly belonging to the Nuns of St. Bridget at Syon. Containing
very curious English rubrics.

UNIVERSITY LIBRARY, Cambridge.—Masses by Dr. Fayrfax, John Taverner, &c. English. Temp. Henry VIII. This and the adjoining MS. (lent by the Master and Fellows of St. John's College, Cambridge) are part books of the same compositions.

ST. PAUL's, The Dean and Chapter.—Psalter and Antiphoner. 14th century.

CANTERBURY, The Archbishop of. — Gradual, English. 16th century. Open at a Gloria, in five parts, composed by Dr. Fayrfax for his Cambridge Degree, 1502.

ST. PETER's COLLEGE, CAMBRIDGE, The Master and Fellows of.—Merbeck. "Ave Dei Patris Filia," in Four Part Volumes. 16th century.

TAPHOUSE, Mr. T. W.—Purcell, Henry. "Hark my Daridcar" (Tyrannick Love). 18th century.

H.M. THE QUEEN.—Tallis, Thomas. Song of 40 parts. Full score, copied in 1751 by John Immyns.

SPENCER, Earl.—Fragments of an Antiphoner. 12th century.

TRINITY COLLEGE, CAMBRIDGE, Master and Fellows of.— Hymns to the Virgin, and secular songs. English and Latin. 15th century.

Wall Case.

SNOECK, Mons. CÉSARE.—*Basset Horn.*
—— *Dulcimer.* 17th century. Antwerp.
—— Collection of fourteen *Flûtes à bec.*
—— *Flûte traversière.* Early 18th century.
—— *Large Clarinet d'Amour*, by Tuerlinckx.
—— *Clarinet*, two keys, by J. B. Willems.
—— *Viola*, by Gaspar Borbon. 1692.
—— *Old Clarinet.* The form suggests the Saxophone.
—— *Large Oboe da Caccia.*
—— *Small Two Keyed Clarinet*, by G. A. Rottenburg.
—— *Small Viola da Gamba*, by J. Willems. 1642.
—— *Large Clarinet d'Amour*, by Rottenburg.
—— *Schalmey.* Netherlandish.
—— *Tenor Viol*, by Pierre Rombouts. 1708.
—— *Tromba Marina*, in metal, with 3 strings. The rose bears the initials D. D. W.
—— *Russian Horn.* 1815.

SNOECK, Mons. CÉSARE.—*Bass Viol,* by Peeter Borbon. About 1641.

—— *Balk,* Norwegian instrument.

—— *Pochette,* by Bernard Sches. 1640 ?

—— *Cornettino,* ivory, engraved. 1697.

—— *Pochette,* by Jean Demaseneer. 17th century.

——   „   „   Guillame de Poilly. 1672.

——   „   „   Hendrik Willems. 1679.

——   „   „   Matthys Hoffmans. 1680.

—— *Zincke,* serpent-shape.

—— *Head of Viol,* by Ambroise de Comble. 1758.

—— *Flûte à bec,* by Rottenburg.

—— *Bass Flûte traversière.*

—— *Bass Flute traversière,* of the largest size, made in Dublin.

—— *Large Trompette à Pistons.*

—— *Keyed Trumpet,* primitive model.

—— *Treble Viol.*

PICTURES, &c.

LAND, Dr., J. P. N.—119. Photograph of Motet-book of St. Peter's Church, Leyden. 1549.

HOBY, Mr. J. C. J.—120. Frame containing three Sketches of Carvings (in stone) from capital in crypt of Canterbury Cathedral and the Choir of Worcester, illustrating ancient musical instruments.

FORT, Mr. C. H. R.—121. Portrait of Bach seated at the organ.

SMALLFIELD, Mr. F.—121*a.* Sketches for four circular panels, painted in oil, for front of a pianoforte.

LAND, Dr. J. P. N.—122. Photograph of Lute-book of Thysius Library, Leyden. 1600.

DICKENS, Mrs. H.—122*a.* Gounod, Charles. Petite pièce d'Orgue composée pour le mariage de sa petite amie Marie Roche. 25 October, 1876.

MOSCHELES, Mr. FELIX.—Mozart, Leopold, Musikalische Schlittenfahrt: Drum part.

ROCHE, Miss OCTAVIE.—Facsimiles of signatures of musicians.

TAPHOUSE, Mr. T. W.—122*b.* Horsley, William. Glee, "O fair eyes." (A. A. T. T. B.)

—— Horsley, William. Round, "Hallelujah."

TAPHOUSE, Mr. T. W.—Croft, Dr. William.   Anthem, "O praise the Lord of Heaven."

MATTHEW, Mr. J. W.—123. Engraving.   Portrait of Beethoven, by Höfel, after Lebronne.   1814.

STEWART, Sir ROBERT.—124. Photograph from a print of Mozart and his children Wolfgang and Nannerl.   About 1766.

DIVISION 22.

Case XLIX.

H.M. THE QUEEN.—Caperario Giovanni (John Cooper), Fantazia almain, &c., written for Charles I., to whom this volume belonged. 17th century.

ASHBURNHAM, Earl of.—Bass part of collection of 164 songs, made by David Melville. 17th century.

DURHAM, The Dean and Chapter of.— Organ part of Services, &c., by Tallis, Bull, Munday, &c., 17th century. Open at "Arise, O Lord" (Tallis), one of the Cantiones Sacrae.
—— Bass of Anthems and Services, by Byrd, Tallis, White, &c. 17th century. Open at Shepherd's "Oh Lord the Maker," sometimes attributed to Henry VIII.
—— Tenor part of Anthems by White Byrd, Giles, &c. 17th century. Open at unpublished Anthems by Gibbons and Byrd.

FITZWILLIAM MUSEUM, Cambridge, The Syndics of the.— Stradella, Alessandro. Score of Oratorio, S. Giovanni Battista. 18th century.

MUSIC, Royal College of.—Lectiones Jeremiae Prophetae Quae Regio in Sacello Cantatur. Written by J. B. Metoyen for Louis XV. 1765.

MARSHALL, Mr. JULIAN.—Italian Cantatas, &c., Anonymous. 17th century.

JACKSON, Mr. J.—Anthems and Services. 18th century. Open at Te Deum, composed for the consecration of the Earl of Oxford's Chapel at Wimpole, 1721, by Dr. Tudway.

H.M. THE QUEEN.—Collections of Canons, &c., by Elway Bevin. 1611. Autograph?

TAPHOUSE, Mr. T. W.—Collection of Dance Tunes in Lute Tablature, by Kühnel, Mouton, Pichler, &c., German. 18th century.

JACKSON, Mr. J.—Purcell Henry. Score of King Arthur's Theatre copy. 18th century.

H.M. THE QUEEN.—Motets in Score by Ferabosco, Tallis, Byrd, Marbeck, Giles, &c. Written by John Baldwin, of Windsor. 1594.
—— A Collection of Puzzle Canons by Bull, Clemens non Papa, &c. 17th century.
—— Will Forster's Virginal Book. 1624.
—— Benjamin Cosyn's Virginal Book, containing lessons, &c., by Bull, Cosyn, &c. 17th century.

CANTERBURY, The Archbishop of.—Cantus part of Services and Anthems by Byrd, Tallis, Gibbons, &c. 17th century.

DURHAM, The Dean and Chapter of.—Contratenor Cantoris of Part Books, containing Preces, Psalms, Anthems and Responses, by Orlando Gibbons, W. Smith, Byrd, Ed. Smith, R. Parsons, Shepperd, &c. Open at unpublished Preces and Responses by Orlando Gibbons. 17th century.

Case L.

KING's COLLEGE, Cambridge, The Provost and Scholars of.—Locke, Matthew. Anthems (four voices), " Let God arise," and " In the beginning, O Lord." Vocal Score.

TAPHOUSE, Mr. T. W.—Hayes, Dr. Philip, " Lady Elizabeth. Spencer's Minuet. Performed in the Maid of Oaks at Blenheim. Compos'd by Dr. Hayes, most humbly inscrib'd to her Grace the Duchess of Marlborough by the author." Full score, dated 12 January, 1788.

MUSIC, The Royal College of.—Greene, Dr. Maurice. Te Deum, Jubilate, Magnificat, and Nunc Dimittis, for three, four, five, six, seven, and eight voices. Vocal score, with figured bass. " Begun at Farnham Castle in May 1737, and finished in London in June following." This copy was bought at Bartleman's sale by Vincent Novello.

KING's COLLEGE, Cambridge, The Provost and Scholars of.—Tudway, Dr., " Thou, O Lord, hast heard our desire." Verse anthem sung to Queen Anne in King's College Chapel on the 16th April, 1705. Vocal score.
—— Croft, Dr. William, Organ part of Anthem " Praise God in the Sanctuary."

MARSHALL, Mr. JULIAN.—Arne, Dr. Thomas Augustine.
Whittington's Feast.' Full score for chorus, orchestra
and solos, the recitatives accompanied by figured bass.

The names of the singers were Mr. Wood, Mrs. Farrel, Mrs. Bartholomew,
and Miss Weller. This volume formerly belonged to William Goodwin and
to the Society of British Musicians.

H.M. THE QUEEN.—Purcell, Henry. Odes, Anthems, and
Welcome Songs, for voices and instruments. Full
score. 1681, &c.

TAPHOUSE, Mr. T. W.—Purcell, Henry. Compositions, open
at an ingenious Canon in two parts.

WESTMINSTER, The Dean and Chapter of.—Blow, Dr.
John. Cupid and Adonis. A Masque. Full score.

MUSIC, The Royal College of.—Croft, Dr. William. Te
Deum, in D major, for orchestra, chorus and solos.
Full score. The solos are for Elford, Barnes, Hughes,
Lee, and Church. Circa 1710.

LUCCA, Signor FRANCESCO.—Balfe, W. M., "Il Passo della
Marna." Tarsa. Full score, dated Venice, 12 November,
1832.

TRINITY COLLEGE, Cambridge, The Master and Fellows
of.—Walmisley, Dr. Thomas Attwood. Installation
ode, for solos, orchestra, and chorus. Full score.

TAPHOUSE, Mr. T. W.—Bishop, Sir Henry Rowley. Ballet
Music. Full score. Dated 1816.
—— Pierson, Henry Hugo. Hymn, "We march to the
House of God," for tenors and basses, with piano accom-
paniment. Dated Würzburg, 15 November, 1858.
—— Crotch, Dr. William. Rounds, Chants, copies of
Italian Madrigals, &c. The Rounds were written in
July, 1816.
—— Cooke, T. Glee (A. T. T. B.) and chorus, "Harmony,"
vocal score.
—— Horsley, William. Madrigal (A. T. T. T. B.), " While
sighing forth his wrongs."
—— Wesley, Dr. S. Single and Double Chants in score.
Dated 2 April, 1800.

LIVERPOOL FREE LIBRARY, The.—Wainwright, Dr. Te
Deum and Jubilate in D major, for orchestra, chorus
and solos. Full score.

LIVERPOOL FREE LIBRARY, The.—Bishop, Sir Henry Rowley. A Volume of Additional Accompaniments (mostly for trombones, horns, and drums) added by Bishop to Overtures by Mozart (Don Juan, Clemenza di Tito, Nozze di Figaro), Beethoven (Egmont), and many others.
—— Bishop, Sir Henry Rowley. Volume of Miscellaneous Scores, containing incidental music to "Love's Labour Lost." 1839.

MARSHALL, Mr. JULIAN.—Travers, John, and Barrow, Thomas. Motets and Anthems for four or five voices, in vocal score, with figured bass accompaniment. 1732–34.

SQUIRE, Mr. W. BARCLAY.—Wesley, Charles. Bass Part of Anthem for the Second Sunday after Easter.

.—Autograph letter of Dr. Burney.

Case LI.

LUCCA, Signor FRANCESCO.—Leo, Leonardo. Pange Lingua, for double chorus and orchestra (incomplete).
—— Paiesiello, Giovanni. Gradual ; 'Omnes de Saba Vanient.' For four voices and organ.
—— Tartini, Giuseppe. Studies and Exercises for the Violin.
—— Zingarelli. Annibale in Torino. Opera in three acts. Full score.

MOSCHELES, Mrs.—Haydn, Joseph. Scena; ' Berenice che fai.' Written in London in 1795, for Banti. Full score.

MUSIC, The Royal College of.—Clari Giovanni Carlo Maria. Mass for four voices and orchestra. Full score. Dated Pistoria, 1725.

MOSCHELES, Mr. FELIX.—Haydn, Joseph. Adante from the Surprise Symphony. Full score.

FITZWILLIAM MUSEUM, Cambridge, The Syndics of the. —Haydn, Joseph. Symphony in F major. Full score.

—— Steffani, Agostino. Motets for voices and organ. 1673-1674.

LIVERPOOL FREE LIBRARY, The. — Galuppi, Baldassar. Vespers, for voices and instruments (incomplete). Full score. In the Autograph of Joseph Haydn.

MAITLAND, Mr. J. A. FULLER.—Galuppi, Baldassar. Venere al Tempio. Cantata for four voices and instruments. Composed for the wedding of two members of the Pisani family, 1775.

—— Durante, Francesco. Thirty-six Ripartimenti, arranged by Mariano Stecher. At the beginning of the volume is a Fragment in Durante's Autograph.

MARSHALL, Mr. JULIAN.—Scarlatti, Alessandro. Cantatas, Duets, &c. At the beginning of the volume is a Duet, 'Luci belle,' in the Composer's Autograph.

GOLDSCHMIDT, Mr. and Mrs. OTTO. — Beethoven's Will. Found amongst his papers after his death.

MOSCHELES, Mr. FELIX.—Beethoven, Ludwig von. Last letters to Ignaz Moscheles, in the handwriting of Anton Schindler. Open at the letter dated the 18th March, 1827, thanking the Philharmonic Society for the £100 sent on account of the proceeds of a concert to be given for Beethoven's benefit.

HUEFFER, Mr. FRANCIS.—Mendelssohn Bartholdy, Felix. Letter to W. Von   . Dated Leipzig, 4th December, 1839, indorsed with an introduction to Clara Wieck (Mdme. Schumann), written by Robert Schumann.

MOSCHELES, Mr. FELIX. — Mendelssohn Bartholdy, Felix. Songs without words, Book I. (Op. 30). The Manuscript is entitled "Melodies for the Pianoforte alone," and dated 10th July, 1832.
—— Mendelssohn Bartholdy, Felix, and Moscheles, Ignaz. Fantasia and Variations on Weber's Preciosa for two pianos and orchestra. Full score.

—— Mendelssohn Bartholdy, Felix, Sestet (Op. 88), by Ignaz Moscheles, arranged for the pianoforte for four hands. Dated August, 1833.
—— Beethoven, L. von. Sketches for the Quartett in C minor (first movement air, variations and finale).
—— Beethoven, L. von. Sketches, chiefly for the Mass in D.

This volume was given by Aloys Fuchs to Mendelssohn on 16th September, 1830, and by Mendelssohn to Moscheles on 19th October, 1832.

—— Bach, Johann Sebastian. Passacaglia for the organ.

DUNCAN, Mr. G. CUTHBERTSON.—Paganini Nicolo. Method of fingering double stopping, communicated to his friend, L. G. Germi.

Roche, Miss Octavie.—Beethoven, Ludwig von. Canon.

Davy, Mr. G. B.—Mozart, W. H. Quintett in D major for two violins, two violas, and violoncello.

Plowden, Miss.—Beethoven, L. von. Sonata for pianoforte and violin in G major.
—— Mozart, W. A. Six Quartets, dedicated to Joseph Haydn. The first is dated Vienna, 31st December, 1792; the remaining five are undated.
—— Mozart, W. A. Three Quartets, dedicated to the Queen of Prussia.
—— Mozart, W. A. Quartet in D major.

Taphouse, Mr. T. W.—Mozart, W. A. Cadenza for a pianoforte concerto.

H.M. The Queen,—Mozart, W. A. "Die Schuldigkeit des ersten und grossten Gebotes." The first part of this Oratorio was written by Mozart at Salzburg at the age of ten (see Jahn. I. 53).

Cummings, Mr. W. H.—Bach, Johann Sebastian. Preludium.
—— Bach, Johann Sebastian. Fragment of an air (bass) from Cantata " Ein feste Burg."

Goldschmidt, Mr. Otto. — Mozart, Wolfgang Amadeus. Concerto in C minor, for pianoforte and orchestra. Full score. Composed in Vienna, March 1786.

Case LII.

Cummings, Mr. W. H.—Bach, John Christian. Cantata a tre voce, "Cefalo e Procri." Dated London, 1776.

Grove, Sir George.—Schumann, Robert. Four part song, "Droben Stehet die Capelle." Autograph of Clara Schumann on the first page.
—— Letter to Diabelli.
—— Autograph MS., by Beethoven.

Davy, Mr. G. B.—Beethoven, L. von. Letter to his brother, and Note Book.
—— Beethoven L. von. Adagio and Fugue from Pianoforte Sonata. (Op. 110.)
—— Beethoven, L. von. Book of Sketches for Sonata for Piano and Violoncello. Op. 102. No. 2.
—— Beethoven, L. von. Scotch and Irish Songs (Op. 108), with violin and violoncello obligato.

GROVE, Sir GEORGE.—Schubert, Franz. Symphony in G major. Dated August, 1821. The full score is unfinished, but the work is sketched throughout.
—— Beethoven's letter to Steiler.

ROCHE, Miss NINA.—Chopin, Frederic. Three studies for the pianoforte.

H.M. THE QUEEN.—Cherubini, Luigi. Motet for Septuagesima. 'Ajutor in oportunitatibus,' for chorus, solo, and orchestra. Dated Paris, 1818.

ORLANDINI, Mdme. M. MORIANI.—Bellini Vincenzo. Letter to Alexander Lanari (27th June, 1834).
—— Bellini Vincenzo. Full score of "Norma."

LUCCA, Signor FRANCESCO.—Donizetti Gactano. Six nocturnes for two violins, viola, flute, two horns, and double bass.
—— Verdi Giuseppe. Il Corsaro, Opera in three Acts. Full score.

CUMMINGS, Mr. W. H.—Bach, Wilhelm (1759–1845). Concerto Buffa, for Bass Solo Orchestra and Toy Instruments. Full score.

ASHBURNHAM, The Earl of.—Rosseau, Jean Jacques. Recueil d'airs avec accompagnement de guitarre.

MOSCHELES, Mr. FELIX.—Moscheles, Ignaz. Studies for the pianoforte.
—— Moscheles, Ignaz. Beatrice di Tenda. Full score.
—— Moscheles, Ignaz. Concerto in G minor, Op. 60. Pianoforte part.

TAPHOUSE, Mr. T. W. — Neukomm, Sigismund, Missa. Brevis for three equal voices, with organ ad lib. score, dated Ardwick Green, 25th July, 1836.

WILLMOTT, Miss.—Dussek, J. L. Corcerto for harp and orchestra. Composed at Chelsea for Mdme. Krumpholz, in July, 1789.

———

DUNCAN, Mr. J. CUTHBERTSON.—Bust of Nicolo Paganini.

PICTURES.

OXFORD, UNIVERSITY OF.—125. Portrait of Charles Frederic Abel.

—— 126. Life-size Portrait of Dr. Child.

MUSICIANS, Royal Society of.—127. Life-size Portrait of George III., by Thomas Gainsborough, R.A. Presented by His Majesty to the Royal Society of Musicians.

OXFORD, UNIVERSITY OF.—128. Life-size Portrait of Dr. Boyce.

—— 129. Portrait of Thomas Tudway.

DIVISION 23.

Case LIII.

SPENCER, Earl.—Missale mixtum secundum regulam Beati Isidori dictum Mozarabes. Folio Toledo. Peter Hagembach. 1500.

—— Missale Moguntiae. Folio. Mainz. Fust and Schöffer. 1483.

—— Psalmorum Codex. Folio. Mainz: Johannes Fust et Petrus Schöffer. 1457.

The famous Mentz Psalter : the first book printed with a date and printer's name.

CRACOW, UNIVERSITY LIBRARY. — Missale Cracoviense. Maguncie, per Petrum Schoiffer de Gernszheijm. Folio. 1487.

—— Missale Cracoviense. Moguntie. Impressum, per Petrum Schoiffer de Gernzheijm. Folio. 1484.

—— Missale Cracoviense. Nurmberge, per Georgium. Stuchs X. Sultzbach. 4to. Circa 1500.

CUMMINGS, Mr. W. H.—Agenda moguntinense (Petrus Schoeffer, circa 1485 ?)

LITTLETON, Mr. A. H.—Psalter and Hymnal. 4to. 147-.

MALINES, THE ARCHIEPISCOPAL SEMINARY OF.—Missale Strigoniense. Small 4to. Venice. Liechtenstein. 1513.

—— Missale Coloniense. Small folio. Basel. 1487.

NATIONAL HUNGARIAN MUSEUM, Buda Pesth. — Missale secundum chorum aline ecclesie Strigoniensis. Impressum Venetiis per Erhardum Ratdolt de Angusta. Folio. 1486.

—— Missale secundum ritum dominorum Ultramontanorum. Impressum Verone. 1480. A. C. S. U. Folio.

—— Missale Strigoniense. Folio. 1481.

—— Missale secundum veram rubricam sacre ecclesie Strigonienses. Impressum Brunne per Conradum Stabel et Maheum Preinlin, impressores Venetos. 1491. Folio.

—— Missale divinorum officiorum secundum chorum alme ecclesie Strigoniensis. Impressum Nurnberge per Georgium Stüchs de Salczpach. 1490. 4to.

Case LIV.

SPENCER, Earl.—Missale Pataviense. Folio. Auguste: Erhardus Ratdolt. 1494.
—— Missale Fratrum Predicatorum. Folio. Venetiis. Andreas de Torresanis de Asula. 1496.
—— Missale Romanum. Folio. Venetiis. Johannes Hammani (Hertzog) de Landoia, 1488.
—— Missale Monasticum secundum consuetudinem ordinis Vallis Umbrosae. Folio. Venitiis: Lucantonius de Giunta. 1503.
—— Missale Herbipolense. Folio. Herbipoli (Würzburg): Georgius Reyser. 1499.
—— Missa de Requiem. Small folio. Vienna: Joannes Winterberg. 1499.
—— Missale Salisburgense. Folio. Nuremberg: Stöchs of Sulczbach. 1498.

WEALE, Mr. W. H. J.—Liber agendorum save Benedictionum secudum ritum ecclesie Bambergensis. Bamberge. Industria ac impensis laurencii Sensenschmidt Johannis Pfeyl et Heinrici Petzensteiner. 1491. 4to.
—— Speciale Missarum secundum usum Moguntinensis ecclesiae. Spiris per Petrum Drach. 1500. Folio.
—— Missale Halberstaltense, sine loco et anno. Circa 1500. Folio.
—— Missale secundum veram rubricam et ordinarum ecclese Mindensis. Nurnberge. In officina Georgii Stuchs, ex Sultzbach. 1513. Folio.

JENKINSON, Mr. F.—Processionale Sarisburiense. 15th century.

BRADSHAW, Mr. HENRY.—Missale ad usum Sarum. Venetiis: Johannes Hamman dictus Hertzog. 1494. 8vo.

LITTLETON, Mr. A. H.—Missale Ordinis Fratrum Praedicatorum. 4to. Venice: A. Scotus. 1482.
—— Agenda Parochialium Ecclesiarum. Small folio. Basel: M. Wenssler and Jacobus de Kilchen. 1488.

Case LV.

WEALE, Mr. W. H. J.—Missale Ratisponense Augusti Vindelicorum sumptibus Jorgi Ratdolt. 1515. 4to.
—— Missale Pragense. Nurenberge in Officina Georgii Stuchs ex Sulczbach. 1503. Folio.

G

JACKSON, Mr. J.—Missale Trajaectense. Small folio. Paris: Hopylius. 1515.

ANDERSON'S COLLEGE, GLASGOW, The Trustees of.—Historia Horarum Canonicarum de S. Hieronymo vario carminum genere contexta. Small folio. Augsburg: Erhardt Ratdoldt. 1512.

MATTHEW, Mr. J. E.—Cantorinus Romanus. 8vo. Venetüs Lucantonius de Giunta. 1513.

MALINES, The Archiepiscopal Seminary of.—Missale Trajectense. Small folio. Paris: Hopylius. 1507.

SPENCER, Earl.—Missale ad usum . . . Sarum folio. London: Richard Pynson. 1504.

RIPON, The Dean and Chapter of.—Missale ad usum celeberrime ecclesie Eboracensis. Small 4to. Rouen: G. Bernard and Jac Cousin. 1517.
—— Processionale ad usum . . . ecclesie Eboracensis. Small 4to. Rouen: M. J. Olivier.
—— Manuale insignis ecclesia Eboracensis. Small 4to. London: Wynkn de Worde. 1509.

ANDERSON'S COLLEGE, GLASGOW, Trustees of.—Processionarium ordinis fratrum praedicatorum rursus recognitum. Small 4to. Venice: Guinta. 1509.

CORPUS CHRISTI COLLEGE, CAMBRIDGE, The Master and Fellows of.—Manuale ad usum Sarum. Small folio. London: R. Pynson. 1506. Printed on vellum.

MUSIC, The Royal College of.—Missale Ratisponense. Folio. Babenbergae (Bamberg): Johannes Pfeyl. 1518.

WELCHMAN, Mr. C. W.—Pontificale Romanum Lugguni per Magistrum Joannem Moilim, alias De Cambray. 1511. Folio.

TRINITY COLLEGE, CAMBRIDGE, Master and Fellows of.— Antiphonarium ecclesiae Sarisburiensis. Pars Hyemalis (Parisiis Wolfgang Hopylius. 1519.) Folio.

MUSIC, ROYAL COLLEGE OF.—Missale Ratisponense. Folio.

WEALE, Mr. W. H. J.—Missale H. Alberstattense, cum proprio Verdense. Luneborck, apud Joannem Heyst. 1511. Folio.

NATIONAL HUNGARIAN MUSEUM, Buda Pesth. — Missale
secundum Chorum almi episcopatus Zagrabiensis
Ecclesie. Venetiis excussum in officina Petri Liechtenstein. Sumptibus Johannis Müer. 1511. Folio.

PEMBROKE COLLEGE, CAMBRIDGE, The Master and Fellows
of. — Missale ad usum ecclesie Eboracensis. Folio.
1516.

Case LVI

ROSENTHAL'S ANTIQUARIAT, Munich.—Cantorinus et Pro-
cessionarius Congregationis Cassinensis. 8vo. Venetiis:
Lucantonius Junta. 1535.

WEALE, Mr., W. H. J.—Missale Romanum. Cesaraugusti.
Georgius Coci, Theutonicus. 1548. 4to.
—— Missale ad usum Romanum. Pari-ii. Per Francis-
cum Regnault. 1530. 8vo.

ROSENTHAL'S ANTIQUARIAT, Munich.—Holthusius, Johannes.
Compendium cantionum ecclesiasticorum. 12mo.
Augsburg : Matheus Francus, 1567.
—— Missale Sarisburiense. Folio. Antwerpie : Christo-
phorus Ruremondensis (Waldarfor)ı 1527.

MALINES, The Archiepiscopal Seminary of.—Missale Came-
racense. Folio. Parisiis, Nicolaus Prepositus. 1527.
—— Missale Tornacense. Folio. Antwerpie : Christophorus
Ruremondensis (Waldarfer). 1527.
—— Missale secundum consuetudinem usum ac ritum in-
signis ecclesie Virdunensis. Folio. Paris: Johannes
Amazeur. 1554.

PEMBROKE COLLEGE, CAMBRIDGE, The Master and Fellows
of.—Missale Romanum. Folio. Salamanca: Guillaume
Foquel. 1588.

MALINES, ARCHIEPISCOPAL SEMINARY OF.—Missale Argen-
tinense. Folio. Hagnoe Thomas Anshelm. 1520.
—— Graduale Romanum. Venetiis ex officina Petri
Liechtenstein. 1580. Folio.
—— Missale Romanum. Antwerpiae ex officina Christo-
phori Plantini 1574. Folio.

BODLEIAN LIBRARY, OXFORD, The Curators of.—Proces-
sionale ad usum Sarum. 4to. Rouen: Printed for
Robert Valentine by Richard Hamilton. 1555.
—— Sacerdotale Romanum. 4to. Venice : Guerracos
Fratres. 1576.

CATHOLIC GREGORIAN ASSOCIATION, THE.—Processionale ad
usum, Sarum. 4to. London. 1554.
—— Manuale ad usum, Sarum. 4to. London. 1554.

WALKER, Mr. JAMES.—Sacerdotale ed consuetudinem Sacro
Sancte Ecclesie Romane. 4to. Venice: Peter Liechtenstein, 1567.

MILLARD, Canon.—Latin hymns with music from the "Cen-
tiloquium Sancti Bonaventura." Printed in Paris by
John Petit. 1570.

Case LVIa.

ST. GREGORY'S MONASTERY, Downshire, Prior of.—Anti-
phonale Diurnum, dispositum juxta Breviarium monasti-
cum Tulli Leucorum. Ex offiicina S. Belgrand et
T. Laurentii. 1643. Folio.
—— Antiphonale Monasticum (Paris). E. Typographia
Ludovici, Sevestre. 17th century. Folio.

MECHLIN, Archiepiscopal Seminary of.—Missale Mogun-
tinum, Moguntiae, excudebat, Balthasarus Lippius.
1602. Folio.
—— Psalterium Cisterciense. Coloniae, sumptibus Henrici
du Sauget. 1723. Folio.

SHREWSBURY, Bishop of.—Missale Romanum. Coloniae
Agrippinae, Sumptibus cornelii ag Egmondt et Sociorum.
1629.

CATHOLIC GREGORIAN ASSOCIATION.—Guaduale Cisterciense.
Lutet ae Parisiorum, ex aedibus Leonardianis. 1696.
Folio.

SHREWSBURY, Bishop of.—Graduale Romanum. Venetiis.
Ex Typographia Balleomana. 1734. Folio.

Wall Case .

SCHUERLEER, Mons. T. F.—*Harp*, Vernis Martin. About
1750.

ERARD, S. & P.—*Harp*. Patented 1811. Showing the first
perfected double action, with a continued outside and
inside movement. The decoration is copied from Her
Majesty's piano in this collection.

AMHERST, Mr. W. A., M.P.—*Harp*, by Consineau Pere et Fils. Carved and painted.

MOLLOY, Mr. FITZGERALD.—*Harp*, Irish.

CORRER, Count GIOVANNI.—*Spinetta, verticale*, Italian, late 15th century. Painted and showing a calvary inside, also a flamboyant window in the soundboard.

ROSENTHAL'S ANTIQUARIAT, MUNICH.—Antiphonarium secundum ordinem sanctae Romanae ecclesiae. Folio. Venice: Lucantonius de Giunta 1499-1500.

WEBER, Rev. G. V., MENTZ.—Extractus Antiphonarii. Moguntiae, typio Francisci Sausen. 1872. Folio.

A reprint in facsimile of the edition of 1673, executed at the expense of the late Sir John Sutton of Norwood Park, for his choral foundation at Kiederich in the Rheingau.

—— Graduale Missali Romano cantui vero Gregoriano Moguntino accomodatum, Moguntiae, typio Francisci Sansen. 1870. Folio.

A reprint in facsimile of the edition of 1671, executed at the expense of the late Sir John Sutton, of Norwood Park, for his choral foundation at Kiederich in the Rheingau.

———

SMART, Miss.—Bust of Carl Maria von Weber. From a cast taken immediately after his death. 5th June, 1826.

ROBERTSON, Mr. W. W.—Two *Kettle Drums*.

PICTURES.

LITTLETON, Mr. HENRY.—130. Portrait of Arne, by Zoffany, R.A.

BROWN, Mr. J. J.—131. Oil Painting, by Mulready, "Tired Out."

MOSCHELES, Mr. FELIX.—132. Portrait of Felix Mendelssohn Bartholdy.

KIRKMAN, Mr.—133. Portrait of Jacob Kirckman (founder of the House of Kirkman & Son), by Hogarth.

SMART, Miss.—134. Portrait of Carl Von Weber, by John Cawse.

CLACY, Miss E.—135. Water Colour Drawing of the Organ Room at Knole Park.

DIVISION 24.

Case LVII.

OUSELEY, REV. Sir F. A., Bart.—Patrocinium Musices. Primus Tomus (Munich. Adam Berg). 1589. Folio.

H.M. THE QUEEN.—Geist- und Lehr-reiches Kirchen- und Haus-Buch. 4to. Dresden: Christopher Matthesius. 1694.

ATKINSON, Mr. JAMES.—Thomas Sternhold and John Hopkins. The whole booke of Psalmes. Folio. London: for the company of Stationers. 1615.

CATHOLIC GREGORIAN ASSOCIATION.—Breviaire Romain noté selon un nouveau système de chant. 12mo. Paris: Quillan. 1727.

BOHMER, Mr. H. B. — Chytraeus Nathan. Psalmorum Davidis Paraphasis Poëtica Georgii Buchanani Scoti. 16mo. Herborn, 1602.

TAPHOUSE, Mr. T. W.—L. (owe·, E. (dward). A Review of some short directions for Performance of Cathedral Service. 8vo. Oxford: W. Hall. 1664.

KING'S COLLEGE, CAMBRIDGE, The Provost and Scholars of.—The whole Psalter translated into English Metre (Archbishop Parker's Version). 4to. London: John Daye, circa 1560.
—— Sternhold, Thomas, Hopkins, John. The whole Booke of Psalmes. Folio, London: John Day. 1576.
—— The Psalmes of David in Prose and Metre: with the whole Forme and Discipline and Prayers, according to the Church of Scotland. 8vo. Aberdene: Edward Raban. 1633.

ST. PAUL'S, Dean and Chapter of.—Sternhold, T., and Hopkins, J. The whole Booke of Psalmes. 12mo. London: for the Company of Stationers. 1622.

TAPHOUSE, Mr. T. W.—Ravenscroft, Thomas. The whole Booke of Psalmes. 12mo. London: for the Company of Stationers. 1621.

—— Tailour, Robert. Sacred Hymns. 4to. London: Thomas Snodham. 1615.

—— X Sondry Authors. The whole Booke of Psalmes with their wonted tunes. 12mo. London: Thomas Est, the assigne of William Byrd, 1594.

HUISH, Mr. M. B.—Sternhold, T., Hopkins, J., and Whittingham, W. The whole Booke of Psalmes. 18mo. London: Imprinted for the Company of Stationers. 1630. Bound up in embroidered covers with the New Testament.

CANTERBURY, The Archbishop of.—Sternhold, Thomas, and Hopkins, John. The Psalmes of David. 12mo. London: Thomas Vautrollier. 1587.

LITTLETON, Mr. A. H.—Contratenor Secundus of Morning and Evening Prayer and Communion, set forthe in foure partes, to be song in churches. (Queen Elizabeth's Prayer noted). Folio. London: John Day. 1565.

—— Marot, Clement, and Betze, Theodore de Pseaumes. 12mo. Pierre Davantes. 1560.

—— The Order of Daily Service. 4to. London: James Burns, 1843.

ST. PAUL's, Dean and Chapter of.—Sterneholde, and others. Four Score and Seven Score Psalmes. 12mo. Geneva: Zacharie Durant. 1561.

H.M. THE QUEEN.—Souter Liedekens. 8vo. Antwerp; Symon Cock. 1540.

BODLEIAN LIBRARY, OXFORD, The Curators of the.—Merbecke, John. The Book of Common Prayer, noted. 4to. London: Richard Grafton, 1550. Edward VI.'s first Prayer Book.

ANDERSON'S COLLEGE, GLASGOW.—"Ein hubsch new Gesangbuch, darinnen begrieffen die Kirchenordnung | unnd geseng | die zür Lants Kron | und Fulneck inn Behern, von der Chrystlychen Bruderschafft den Piccarden | die bisshero für unchristen | und Ketzer gehalten | gebraucht unnd teglich Gott zu ehren gesungen werden." Ob. 8vo. Ulm: Hans Varnier. 1538.

This volume belonged successively to J. S. Bach, C. P. E. Bach, Dr. Burney, J. Stafford Smith, and the Rev. W. H. Havergal.

Case LVIII.

ROSENTHAL'S ANTIQUARIAT, Munich.—Psalmorum select-
orum a praestantissimis hujus nostri temporis in Arte
musica artificibus in harmonias IV., V., et VI., vocum
redactorum Quatuor Tomi (Tenor Pars). ob. 8vo.
Nürnberg, J. Montanus et U. Neuber. 1553–54.
—— Barberius, Melchior. Intabulatura di Lautto di Fan-
taisie, Lib. X. Ob. 4to. Venice: Hieronymus Scotus.
1549.
—— Borrono, Pietro Paolo. Intavolatura di Lauto, Libro VIII.
Ob. 8vo. H. Scotus. 1548.
—— Rotta, Antonio. Intabolatura de Lauto. Libro I.,
ob. 8vo. Venice. 1546.

MUSIC, The Royal College of.—Heckel, Wolff. Lautten Buch.
ob. 8vo. Strasbourg: Christian Müller. 1562.

LITTLETON, Mr. A. H.—Gervaise, Claude. Quart. Livre
Contenant XXVI., Chansons Musicales à troys parties.
Ob. 8vo. Paris: Attaignant. 1550.

ANDERSON'S COLLEGE, GLASGOW, Trustees of.—Macrope-
dius, Georgius. Pretiscus. Sm. 8vo. Utrecht: Har-
mannus Bolculous. 1553.
—— Macropedius, Georgius. Lazarus. Sm. 8vo. Utrecht,
n. d.
—— Arcadelt, G. Il terzo libro di Madrigali. Ob. 8vo.
Venice: Gardano. 1543.
—— Senfi Ludwig Varda Carminum, Geneva. Ob. 8vo.
Nunberg. Hieronymus Formschneider, 1534.

LITTLETON, Mr. A. H.—Xistus, Theodoricus. Magnificat
octo tonorum Liber Primus. Ob. 8vo. Strasburg:
Peter Schoeffer, 1535.
—— Animuccia, Joannes. Missarum Liber Primus. Folio.
Rome: Haeredes Valerii et Alzoii Doricorum Fratrum,
1567.
—— Senfi Ludwig, Liber Selectarum Cantionum quas Vulgo
Mutetas appellant sex quinque et quatuor Vocum.
Folio, 1520.
—— Verardus Marcellinus. Caesenatis Elegia, 8vo. Rome:
Fucharius Silber alias Franck. 1493.

SPENCER, Earl.—Higden, Ranulph. Polychronicon En-
gylsshed, by Syr Johan de Trevysa. Sm. folio.
Westminster: Wynkyn de Worde. 1495.

H.M. THE QUEEN.—Borchgrevinck Melchior Giardino Novo. 4to. Copenhagen: Hen. Waltkirch. 1606.

JACKSON, Rev. J. C.—Wilbye, John. The Second Set of Madrigales. 4to. London : Thomas Este, alias Snodham. 1609.

ANDERSON'S COLLEGE, GLASGOW, The Trustees of.—Kapsberger, Girolamo. 'Libri Primo de Madrigali.' 8vo. Rome: Pietro Manelfi. 1608.

H.M. THE QUEEN.—Le Jeune Claude. Le Printemps. Ob. 8vo. Dessus, Paris Ballard. 1603.
—— Mundy, John. Songs and Psalms. 8vo. London : Thomas Este (the Assigne of William Byrd). 1594.
—— Palestrina, G. P. Missae. 8vo. Venice : Herede di Gerolamo Scotto. 1585.
—— Byrd William and Tallis Thomas. Musica Transalpina. Part I. Cantus. 8vo. Loudon : Thomas East, the Assigne of Wm. Byrd. 1588.
—— Byrd William and Thomas Tallis. Cantiones, quae ab argumento Sacrae vocantur, quinque et sex partium. Ob. 8vo. London: Thomas Vautroller. 1575.

JACKSON, Rev. J. C.—Coler Val Liber Primus. Cantionum Sacrarium Cantus. 4to. Ober-Ursel. Cornelius Sutor, for J. L. Britich. 1604.
—— Byrd, William. Songs of Sundrie Natures. Bassus. 8vo. London: Thomas Este, the Assigne of Wm. Byrd. 1589.

MUSIC, The Royal College of,—Holborne, Antony and William. 'The Cittharn Schoole.' London: Peter Short, 1597.

ROSENTHAL'S ANTIQUARIAT, Munich. — Byrd, William. 'Liber Primus Sacrarum Cantionum Superius.' 8vo. London : Thomas East. 1589.

JACKSON, Rev. J. C.—Knefel, Joannes. Dulcissimae quaedam. Cantiones, Altera pars. Ob. 8vo. Nürnberg, Theodor Cerlatz. 1571.

ROSENTHAL'S ANTIQUARIAT, Munich. — Joannelli, Petrus Bergomensis Novi atque Catholici Thesauri musici. Lib. I.-V. (Quinta Pars). 4to. Venice: Gardano. 1568.

CUMMINGS, Mr. W. H.—Pierre de la Rue. Missale. Ob.
8vo. Venice : Ottario Petrucci, 1503.

MILLARD, Canon.—Gerson, J. Collectorium super Magnificat. Folio (Strasburg, H. Eggesteyn ?). 1473.

This volume is opened at what is believed to be the first example of printed
musical notation. The emotions of joy, hope, pity, fear, and grief are represented by a descending scale of notes, probably intended to be connected by
a stave of five lines ruled in red ink by hand.

SAVENAU, Baron VON.—Photograph of the title-page of
Lazin's Typi Chorographici. Vienna. 1561. Folio.

Case LIX.

CUMMINGS, Mr. W. H.—Johann Sebastian Bach. Die Kunst
der Fuge. 1752. Ob. Folio. Leipzig.

—— Johann Sebastian Bach. Musicalisches opfer Sr.
Königlichen Majestat in Prussen, &c. Unterthanigst
gewidmet. Ob. folio. Engraved by J. G. Schubler.
Leipzig. 1749.

—— Johann Sebastian Bach. Clavier-Uebung bestehend
in einer Aria mit verschiedenen Veraenderungen vors
Clavicembal mit Manualen denen Liebhabern zur
Gemüths Ergetzung verfertigt. Folio. Nürnberg :
Balthazar Schmids, *n. d.*

- —— Johann Sebastian Bach. Dritter Theil der Clavier
übung bestehend in verschieden Vorspielen über die
Catechismus und andere Gesaenge, vor die Orgel :
Denen Liebhabern, und besonders denen Kennern von
dergleichen Arbeit, zur Geuiüthe Ergezung verfertiget.
Ob. folio. Leipzig : In verlegung des Autoris 1727.
Engraved on copper by Bach himself.

—— Johann Sebastian Bach. Einige canonische Veraenderungen uber das Weynacht-Lied ' Von Himmel hoch
da komm ich her.' Vor die Orgel mit 2 clavieren und
dem Pedal. Folio. Nürnberg : Balthazar Schmids, n.d.

LITTLETON, Mr. A. H.—Frescobaldi Girolamo. Toccate e
Partite d' Intavolatura. Libro Primo. Rome : Nicolo
Borbone. 1618.

H.M. THE QUEEN.—Gesualdo, Carlo, Prince of Venosa.
Partitura delli sei libri de Madrigali. 8vo. Genoa :
Guiseppe Pavoni. 1613.

—— Bach, C. P. Exempel nebst achtzehn Probe Stücken
in sechs Sonaten zu Carl Philipp Emanuel Bachs.
Versuch über die wahre Art das Clavier zu Spielen
auf 26 Kupfer Tafeln. Imp. folio. Berlin : S. L.
Winter. 1759.

H.M. the QUEEN.—Byrd, Bull and Gibbons. 'Parthenia, or the Maydenhead of the first Musicke that ever was printed for the Virginalls.' Folio. Engraved by William Hold for Dorothy Evans. London: G. Lowe (1611).

ANDERSON'S COLLEGE, Glasgow, The Trustees of.—Kapsberger, Girolamo. Libro Primo di Mottetti Passegiati a' una Voce. Raccolto dal Signor Francesco de Nobili. Folio. Rome, 1612.

—— Ford, Thomas. Musicke of sundrie kindes, set forth in two bookes. Imp. folio. London: John Windet and the Assignes of William Barley. 1607.

RESSE, Count PIO DE.—Peri Jacopo. Le Musicke Sopra l' Euridice del Sig. Ottavio Rinuccini. Folio. Florence : Giorgio Marescotti. 1600.

TAPHOUSE, Mr. T. W.—Frescobaloci, Girolamo. Toccate d' Intavolatura. Libro Primo. Rome: Niccolo Borbone. 1637.
—— Couperin, L'Art de Toucher le Clavecin. Paris. Engraved by Berey. 1717.
—— Locke Matthew Melothesia. London: J. Carr, 1673.

MATTHEW, Mr. J. E.—Leclair. Premier Livre de Sonates a Violon. Paris. Engraved by L. Hue. 1723.

MAITLAND, Mr. J. A. FULLER.—Handel, G. F. Suites de pieces pour le Clavecin. London: J. Walsh. 1740.

MUSIKFREUNDE, The Gesellschaft der, Vienna. — Muffat-Theofilo. Componimenti Musicali per il Cembalo. Vienna: G. C. Leopold. 1727.

BARTHOLOMEW, Mrs. MOUNSEY.—Musick Engraved by G. Bickham, Jun. London. 1737.

MARSHALL, Mr. JULIAN.—Purcell, Henry. Sonnatas of three parts. London: Printed for the Author. Engraved by Thomas Cross, Jun. 1683.

DAWS, Mr. CHARLES.—Purcell, Henry. A Collection of Ayres, compos'd for the Theatre, and upon other occasions. Violino Primo. London: J. Heptinstall. 1697.

H.M. THE QUEEN.—Amaryllis. Vol. 1. London : Thomas Jefferys. 1738.
—— De la Borde. Choix de Chansons. Paris : Engraved by Moria and Mdle. Vendome. 1773.

Case LX.

Musikfreunde, The Gesellschaft der, Vienna.—Coclaeus
Johannes. Tetrachordum Musices. 8vo. Nürnberg:
Johannes Stuchssen. 1512.
—— Faber, Jacobus. Elementa Musicalia. 8vo. Paris:
Henri Stephan. 1514.
—— Britig, Hans Judenkunig. Ein Schone kunstliche under-
weisung in disem buechlein leychtlich zu begreyffen
den rechten grund zu lernen auff der Lautten und
Geygen. 8vo. Vienna: H. Singrycner. 1523.

Matthew, Mr. J. E.—Glareanus, H. Isagoge in Musicem.
8vo. Basel. 1516.
—— Folianus, L. Musica Theorica. Sm. folio. Venice:
Jo. Antinous et Fratres de Sabio. 1529.
—— Aaron, Peter. Tratatto della Natura et cognitione di
tutti gli Suoni di Canto Figurato. Sm. folio. Venice:
Bernardino di Vitali. 1525.
—— Aaron, Peter. De Institutione Harmonica. 8vo. Bo-
logna: Benedict Hector. 1516.
—— Prasperg, Balthasar. Clarissima plane atque choralis
musice interpretatio. 8vo. Basel: Michael Furter. 1507.
—— Zabern, Jacobus. Ars bene cantandi choralem cantum.
24mo. Mainz: Frederick Hewman. 1509.
—— Spangenberg Johannes. Questiones Musica. 12mo.
Wittenberg: Georg Rhan. 1542.
—— Heyden, Sebaldus. Musicae id est, artis canendi. 4to.
Nürnberg: Joh. Petreins. 1537.
—— Froschius, Johannes Kerum Musicarum Opuscinum.
Sm. folio. Strasburg: Peter Schoeffer et Mathias Api-
arum. 1535.
—— Vanni, S. Recanetum de Musica Aurea. Sm. folio.
Rome: Valerius Doricus Brixiensis. 1533.

Rosenthal's Antiquariat, Munich. — Nachtgall, Othm.
(Luscinius) Musicae Institutiones. 12mo. Strasburg:
Johannes Knoblanch. 1515.
—— Bonaventura de Brixia. Regula Musice. 16mo.
Venice: J. Franc et J. A. de Rusconi. 1524.
—— Faber, Nicholas Musicae rudimenta. 8vo. Augs-
burg: Müller. 1516.
—— Glareanus Dodekachordon. Folio. Basel: Hen. Peters.
1547.
—— [Wollick, Nicholas.] Opus Aureum. 8vo. Cologne:
H. Quental. 1501.
—— Flores Musicae, seu omnis cantus Gregoriani. 8vo.
Strasburg: Pryss. 1488.

LITTLETON, Mr. A. H.—Aaron, Peter Toscanello. Sm. folio.
Venice: Bernardíno et Mattheo de Vitali, 1523.

SPENCER, Earl.—Gaforius Franchinus. De Harmonia musi-
corum Instrumentorum. Sm. folio. Milan: Gothardus
Pontanus. 1518. Bound by Grolier.
—— Burtius, Nicolaus. Op.sculum musices, cu n de-
fensione Guidonis Aretini. 8vo. Bologna: Ugo de
Rugeriis. 1487.
—— Gaforius, Franchinus. Theoricum opus musice dis-
cipline. 8vo. Naples: Franciscus di Dino. 1480.

ANDERSON'S COLLEGE, Glasgow, The Trustees of.—Gafo-
rius, Franchinus. De Harmonia Musicorum Instru-
mentorum. Sm. folio. Milan: Gothardus Pontanus.
1518.
—— Gaforius, Franchinus. Practica Musicae. Folio.
Venice. 1512.
—— Gaforius, Franchinus. Theorica Music. Sm. folio.
Milan: P. Mantegati. 1492.
—— Gaforius, Franchinus. Angelicum ac divinum opus
musice. Folio. Milan: Gothard de Ponte. 1508.
—— Gaforius, Franchinus. Practica Musice. Sm. Folio.
Milan: Guillaume Siguerre. 1496.

TAPHOUSE, Mr. T. W.—Listen ius. Nic. Musica. 12mo.
Fraukfort a/a Oder: Johannes Erchorn. 1550 (?)
—— Musicks Handmaid. London: J. Playford. 1678.
—— Reisch, G. Margarita Philosophica. 4to. Strasburg:
Johannes Grüninger. 1504.

WALKER, Mr. JAMES.—Songs and Fancies to three, four, or
five parts, both apt for Voices and Viols, with a brief
Introduction to Music, as is taught iu the Music School
of Aberdeen: John Forbes. 1682.

LITTLETON, Mr. A. H.—Gaforius, F. Practica Musicae.
Folio. Bresica, Bernadino Misinta de Papia. 1502.

CANTERBURY, The Archbishop of.—Reus, Jacobus. De
Tractatus brevis. 24mo. Antwerp: Gerard Leo.
1491.

Case LXI.

TAPHOUSE, Mr. T. W.—The Modern Musick Master. 8vo.
London. 1780.

TAPHOUSE, Mr. T. W.—Playford, John. A brief introduction
to the Skill of Music. Small 8vo. Unnumbered Edition.
London : W. Goodbid. 1658.

—— Diruta Girolamo. Il Transilvano. Venice : Alessandro
Vincenti. 1625.

—— A Short Explication of such Foreign Words as are
made use of in Music Books. 18mo. London : Brother-
ton. 1724.

—— The Compleat Flute-master. Ob. 8vo. London : H.
Hare and J. Walsh, *n. d.*

ALLEN, Mr. E. HERON.—Recueil de Planches de l'Encyclo-
pédie. 4to. Paris : Panckoucke. 1784.

—— Simpson, Christopher. Chelys, minurit'onum-artificio
exornata. The Division-Viol, or the Art of playing
extempore upon a ground. 2nd edition. Folio. London : W. Goodbid. 1667.

—— Crome, Robert. The Fiddle New Model'd. 8vo.
London : David Rutherford, *n. d.*

—— Rousseau, Jean. Traité de la Viole. 8vo. Paris :
Jean Ballard. 1688.

MUSIC, Royal College of. — Mace, Thomas. Musick's
Monument ; or a Remembrancer of the Best Practical
Musick, both Divine and Civil, that has ever been
known to have been in the World. Folio. London :
T. Radcliffe and N. Thompson. 1676.

—— Dowland, John. Andreas Ornithoparcus ; his Micro-
logus. Sm. folio. London : Thomas Adams. 1609.

—— Caroso Fabritio. Nobiltà di Dame. 4to. Venice :
Presso il Muschio. 1605.

LITTLETON, Mr. A. H.—Valerius, Adriaen. Nederlandtsche
Gedenck-Clank. Ob. 4to. Haerlem : the author's heirs
at Veer, Zeeland. 1626.

—— Agricola, M. Musica Instrumentalis. 12mo. Wittem-
berg : Georg Rhaw. 1529.

—— Nachtigall, Ottomar (Luscinius). Musurgia. Obl. 8vo.
Strasburg : Johann Schott. 1536.

—— Virdung Sebastian. Musica getutscht. Ob. 8vo.
(Basel ?). 1511.

—— Praetorius, M. Syntagma Musicum. 4to. Wittenberg : Johann Richter. 1615. Wolffenbüttel : Elias
Holwein. 1619–1620.

—— Negri, Cesare. Nuove Inventione di Balli. Folio.
Milan : Girolanio Bordone. 1604.

—— Curoso Fabritio. Il Ballarino. 8vo. Venice : Francesco Ziletti. 1581.

MATTHEW, Mr. J. E.—Fludd. De Templo Musicae. Folio.
Oppenhiem. 1617.
—— Artusi G. M. L'Arte del Contrapunto. Sm. folio.
Venice: Giac. Vincenti. 1598.
—— Salinas, F. De Musica. Sm. folio. Salamanca: Math.
Gastias. 1517.
—— Benelli, A. Il Desiderio. 4to. Venice: Rich. Amadino.
1594.
—— Aristoxenus. Harmonicorum Elementorum libri tres.
4to. Venice: Vincenzo Valgrisi. 1562.
—— Gumpelzhaimer, Adam. Compendium Musicæ. 4to.
Augsburg. 1600.
—— Artusi, G. M. L'Artusi. Sm. folio. Venice: Giac
Vincenti. 1600.
—— Marinati, Aurelio. Somma di Tutte le Scienze. 8vo.
Rome: Barth. Bonfadino. 1587.

WALKER, Mr. JAMES. — Bonanni, Filippo. Gabinetto
Armonico. 8vo. Rome: Giorgio Placho. 1722.

ROSENTHAL'S ANTIQUARIAT, Munich. — Lambranzi, G.
Nuova e Curiosa Scuola de Balli. Folio. Nürnburg:
J. J. Wolrab. 1716.
—— Tigrini, Orazio. Il compendio della Musica. 4to.
Venice: Rich. Amadino. 1588.

RICHARDSON, H. J.—Longman & Lukey. Complete pack
of new Cotillons. London.

Case LXII.

CAMBRIDGE, UNIVERSITY LIBRARY.—Mass. English, late
15th century.

ASHBURNHAM, Earl of.—Gradual, music written in Uncial
Notes. 15th century. Italian.

RIPON, The Dean and Chapter of.—Gerson. De Consola-
tione Theologie Cologne. 1488. And other Treatises.

On the blank leaves are written: (a) Copy of letter from John (Auckland)
Prior of Durham to John Portar, 1484; (b) An account of a case of
Demoniacal Possession; (c) "A Ballet of ye deth of ye Cardynall" (i.e.
Wolsey); (d) "A Lytyll Balet Mayde of ye yong dukes grace" (i.e. Henry
Fitzroy, Duke of Richmond and Somerset, died 1536). The two last manu-
scripts are set to three part music.

STONYHURST, The Very Rev. the Rector of.—Collection of
Motets for 4, 5, 6, and 7 voices, by Josquin des Pres,
Clemens non Papa, and others. Pars Quinta and Pars
Septima only. 16th century.

CANTERBURY, Archbishop of.—Processional, 15th century. English.

SALISBURY, Dean and Chapter of.—Tonale ad usum Sarum. Early 14th century. English.

Case LXIII.

CRACOW UNIVERSITY, LIBRARY OF.—Gradual, with Sequences. Hungarian. 15th century. Open at Hungarian Sanctus.

CAMBRIDGE UNIVERSITY LIBRARY.—Lute Music in Tablature. English. 17th century.

ST. JOHN'S COLLEGE, CAMBRIDGE, Master and Fellows of. Antiphoner. 15th century.

On Inner Wall.

MILLARD, Canon.—Portrait of Dr. Wm. Hayes, engraved by Thomas Park, after the painting by John Cornish in the Music School, Oxford.
—— Dr. William Hayes. Autograph Receipt.

MARSHALL, Mr. JULIAN.—Articles of Agreement between Laporte and Rubini. 1833.
—— Autograph Letter of Rubini. 1832.
—— Portrait of Schumann (composer), by Kriehuber. 1839.
—— Medallion of Robert and Clara Schumann.
—— Portrait of Boccherini, by De la Richardiere, after Lefevre.
—— Original Manuscript, by Bach.
—— Portrait of Jullien.
—— Jullien Conducting. Drawing by G. Cruikshank.
—— Portrait of Incledon, by Vendramini, after Barber. 1804.
—— Autograph Letter of Charles Incledon. 1807.
—— Portrait of Purcell, by White, after Clostermann.
—— Portrait of Purcell, from a painting by Clostermann.
—— Portrait of Onslow (composer).
—— Original Manuscript, by Onslow.
—— Portrait of Zingarelli (bust).
—— Original Manuscript, by Zingarelli.
—— Portrait of Sacchini (composer).
—— Original Manuscript, by Sacchini.
—— Original Manuscript, by Bellini.
—— Portrait of Bellini.

MARSHALL, Mr. JULIAN.—Portrait of Paganini, by Cala-
matta, after Ingres. 1818.
—— The "Concert," by St. Aubyn. The boy playing the
violin is the portrait of Mozart. (Drawings.)
—— Portrait of Offenbach, by Laemlein. 1850.
—— Caricature Portrait of Offenbach.
—— Autograph Letter of Offenbach.
—— Bust of Offenbach, with memorial verses.
—— Articles of Agreement between Sheridan and Pac-
chierotti. 1782.
—— Autograph Letter from Paisiello to Talleyrand. 1814.
—— Portrait of Rouget de Lisle, by Lerroux, after David.
1830.
—— Autograph Letter of Rouget de Lisle.
—— Portrait of Beranger, after Scheffer.
—— Autograph Letter of Beranger.
—— Portrait of Cervetto, by Picot, after Zoffany.
—— Document signed by Cervetto.
—— Portrait of Marchesi, by Schiavonetti, after Cosway.
—— Caricature Portrait of Marchesi, by Nixon.
—— Autograph Letter from Pacchierotti to the Rev. W.
Mason. 1780.

PICTURES, ETC.

BRENN, Mr. J. N.—136. Queen Elizabeth and her Court
at Hunsdon House. An early representation of the
Virginals.

CUMMINGS, Mr. W.—137. Portrait of Dr. John Bull. 1628.
139. Portrait of Thomas Whythorne, by John Day.
1571.

OXFORD, UNIVERSITY OF.—138. Portrait of John Bull.

JACKSON, Mr. R.—140. Portraits of Great Musicians, engraved by T. Landseer, after P. J. de Loutherbourg.
London: H. de Janory. 1801.

CATHOLIC GREGORIAN ASSOCIATION.—40A. Fragment of an
Antiphoner. Italian. 15th century.

DIVISION 25.

Screen E.

CHESTER, Mr. JOHN.—Eight Engravings, by various Artists, of St. Cecilia.

DECOA, Mdlle M.—Engraved Portrait of Giulia Grisi.

.—Photograph of two Angels.

FORT, Mr. C. H. K.—Woodcut of an Organ Front.

SCHUERLEER, Herr.— „ representing Festival held by the Prince of Orange in 1686.

WEALE, Mr. W. H. J.—Photographs of two carved Figures.

ALLEN, Mr. E. H.—Caricature of a Violoncello Player.

.—Woodcut, Portrait of Master Mori.

.—Engraving by F. Bartolozzi.

COLNAGHI & Co., Messrs.—Sketch of Paganini, by Sir E. Landseer.

JACKSON, Rev. J. C., M.A. — Sportsman's Handkerchief, Linen, with five engraved subjects and songs. 18th century.
—— Portrait of Miss Harriot Powell.
—— „ Teniers playing the Violoncello, and his family.
—— Coloured Sketch of Mozart and his two children.
—— Woodcut of a Flageolet Player.
—— Print. Four Portraits of Paganini.
—— Coloured Print. Head of a Boy.
—— Coloured Print of Dr. Arne, by F. Bartolozzi.

BOHMER, Mr. H. B.—Portrait of G. Rossini.

HENDERSON, Mr. W.—Three Woodcuts of Old Drury Lane Theatre.
—— *Collection of Playbills, &c :*—
Theatre Royal, Covent Garden, 1826, announcing first appearance of Weber in this country.
Argyll Rooms, 1826, announcing appearance of Weber.
Bartholomew Fair Theatre.

HENDERSON, Mr. W.—*Collection of Playbills, &c.:*—

St. Martin's Lane Theatre.

Ipswich Theatre, 1776, where Garrick first appeared.

Theatre Royal, Drury Lane, 1734, announcing appearance of Mrs. Porter.

Theatre Royal, Drury Lane, 1791, last performance in Wren's theatre.

Theatre Royal, Drury Lane, 1768, with portraits of Garrick.

Theatre Royal, Drury Lane, 1767.

—— Playhouse Bill for Starching.—Signed by Cibber, Wilks, and Booth, 1715.

Screen F.

HENDERSON, Mr. W.—*Collection of Playbills, &c.:*—

Theatre Royal, Covent Garden, 1834, announcing first appearance of Mdlle. Giulietta Grisi in a dramatic character.

Theatre Royal, Covent Garden, 1834, announcing Mdlle. Grisi.

Theatre Royal, Covent Garden, 1834, announcing conductorship of Signor M. Costa.

Theatre Royal, Drury Lane, 1843, announcing first appearance of Clara Novello (afterwards Countess Gigliucci) on the English Stage.

Theatre Royal, Covent Garden, 1781, performance of "The Beggars' Opera," announcing Miss Anne Catley.

Theatre Royal, Strand, 1822, announcing last appearance of Incledon.

Theatre Royal, Covent Garden, 1826, announcing first performance of "Oberon."

Theatre Royal, Drury Lane, 1830, first appearance of Signor Lablache and Signor Santini.

Theatre Royal, Covent Garden, 1833, announcing Madame Pasta.

Theatre Royal, Drury Lane, 1836, announcing Mons. Benedict.

Theatre Royal, Drury Lane, 1829, announcing first appearance of Mdlle. Sontag (Countess Rossé) and her sister Mdlle. Nina Sontag.

Theatre Royal, Drury Lane, 1836, announcing Madame Malibran and Signor Lablache.

New Theatre Royal, Covent Garden, 1782, announcing Signora Giovanna Sestini's first appearance on the English Stage.

HENDERSON, Mr. W.—*Collection of Playbills, &c.*:—
New Theatre Royal, Covent Garden, 1789, announcing
Miss Fontenellé.
New Theatre Royal, Covent Garden, 1784, announcing
the first performance of " Robin Hood," by Shield.
New Theatre Royal, Covent Garden, 1786, announcing
Bellamy, Carter, Pring, and Miss George (after-
wards Lady Oldmixon).
Theatre Royal, Drury Lane, 1791, announcing per-
formance of Handel's oratorio, " Israel in Egypt."
Theatre Royal, Drury Lane, 1791, announcing per-
formance of " Messiah."
Theatre Royal, Drury Lane, 1821, announcing per-
formance of opera of " Rob Roy Macgregor."
Portrait of Mr. Mackay as *Bailie Nicol Jarvey.*
Theatre Royal, Edinburgh, 1824, announcing per-
formance of opera of " Rob Roy Macgregor."
Theatre Royal, Drury Lane, 1789, announcing the
first appearance of Signora Storace on the English
stage.
Theatre Royal, York, 1780, announcing John Kemble's
appearance in comic opera.
Theatre Royal, Drury Lane, 1791, announcing first
performance of Storace's comic opera, " The Siege
of Belgrade."
Theatre Royal, Covent Garden, 1794, announcing
Incledon in " The Gentle Shepherd."
Theatre Royal, Drury Lane, 1824, announcing Mr.
Mackay as *Dominie Sampson* in " Guy Mannering."
Otley Theatre, 1790, announcing the benefit of Miss
Harriet Mellon (afterwards Mrs. Coutts and Duchess
of St. Albans).
Theatre Royal, Covent Garden, 1822, announcing
first appearance at this theatre of Miss Paton
(Lady Lennox, afterwards Mrs. Wood).
Theatre Royal, Drury Lane, 1822, announcing Ed-
mund Kean as *Tom Tug.*
Theatre Royal, Drury Lane, 1818, announcing Master
H. G. Blagrove.
Theatre Royal, Drury Lane, 1831, announcing John
Templeton, " Malibran's Tenor" and " Scottish
Vocalist." (First appearance in London).
Theatre Royal, Lyceum, 1813, announcing Mr. and
Mrs. Cooke and Master Barnett.
Theatre Royal, Covent Garden, 1830, announcing first
appearance of John Wilson on the London stage.

HENDERSON, Mr. W.—*Collection of Playbills, &c. :*—

> Theatre Royal, Drury Lane, 1802, announcing appearance of Mrs. Billington and Mrs. Crouch.

Theatre Royal, Covent Garden, 1813, announcing first appearance of Catherine Stephens (afterwards Countess of Essex).

Theatre Royal, Drury Lane, 1801, announcing first appearance of Mrs. Billington.

Theatre Royal, Drury Lane, 1786, announcing appearance of Miss Farren (afterwards Countess of Derby) " with a song."

Theatre Royal, Drury Lane, 1786, announcing John Kemble in a singing part.

Theatre Royal, Drury Lane, 1789, announcing Mrs. Siddons with a song in character.

King's Theatre, 1829, announcing first appearance of Madame Malibran in an English character.

Theatre Royal, Drury Lane, 1829, announcing first appearance of Madame Malibran Garcia on the English stage.

Theatre Royal, Covent Garden, 1829, announcing first appearance of Mdlle. Sontag and Mdlle. Nina Sontag.

Theatre Royal, Covent Garden, 1788, announcing Leoni's benefit and first appearance of Master Braham as an actor.

Theatre Royal, Drury Lane, 1796, announcing first appearance of John Braham as a tenor singer.

Theatre Royal, Covent Garden, 1787, first appearance of Master Braham on any stage.

Theatre Royal, Covent Garden, 1787, first appearance of Michael Kelly on the English stage.

Theatre Royal, Covent Garden, 1797, announcing appearance of Mrs. Jordan (with a song) and C. B. Incledon.

Theatre Royal, Covent Garden, 1786, announcing first appearance of Mrs. Billington.

Theatre Royal, Drury Lane, 1759, announcing Thos. Lowe and Mrs. Clive at this theatre.

Theatre Royal, Drury Lane, 1760, announcing Master Leoni (afterwards Master of Braham).

Theatre Royal, Covent Garden, 1786, announcing first appearance of James Hooke.

Theatre Royal, Covent Garden, 1816, showing the earliest cast of "Guy Mannering.'

Engraving of Mr. Liston (as the first *Domine Sampson*) by George Cruickshank ?

HENDERSON, Mr. W.—*Collection of Playbills, &c.* :—

Theatre Royal, Covent Garden, 1818, showing the earliest cast of "Rob Roy." Music by Sir H. Bishop and John Davey.

Theatre Royal, Covent Garden, 1797, announcing first appearance of Madame Mara in comic opera.

Theatre Royal, Drury Lane, 1755, announcing John Beard as *Amiens* in "As You Like It."

Theatre Royal, Covent Garden, 1796, announcing first appearance of Madame Mara at Covent Garden.

Theatre Royal, Covent Garden, 1787, announcing first appearance of Mrs. Billington as *Mandane.*

Theatre Royal, Lincoln's-Inn-Fields, 1732, announcing performance of "Flora; or, Hob in the Well."

Theatre Royal, Covent Garden, 1766, announcing Charles Dibdin, John Beard, and Mrs. Pinto.

Theatre Royal, Covent Garden, 1823, announcing a concerto on the violin by Master Balfe.

Theatre Royal, Lyceum, 1813, announcing first appearance of Master Barnett.

Theatre Royal, Drury Lane, 1824, announcing Braham's night and Master Liszt.

Theatre Royal, Covent Garden, 1793, announcing first appearance of Miss Poole (afterwards Mrs. Dickons).

Theatre Royal, Covent Garden, 1755, announcing Mr. Lowe, Mrs. Chambers, and Mrs. Woffington.

Theatre Royal, Covent Garden, 1790, announcing Mrs. Billington's benefit, and her first appearance as *Ophelia.*

Theatre Royal, Covent Garden, 1784, announcing Mrs. Kennedy, Bannister, and Leoni.

Theatre Royal, Covent Garden, announcing Anne Catley and John Beard.

Theatre Royal, Drury Lane, 1779, announcing Webster's benefit.

Theatre Royal, Covent Garden, 1832, announcing Paganini's last concert at Covent Garden.

Theatre Royal, Covent Garden, 1763, announcing a comic mimic Italian song, after the manner of Paganini, by Mrs. Clive.

Theatre Royal, Drury Lane, 1832, announcing Paganini's last appearance at Drury Lane.

Theatre Royal, Adelphi, 1867, first performance of "Cox and Box." (*On Wall of Inner Room from Oriental Room.*)

On Inner Wall.

NORWOOD, Mr. WM.—Portrait of Mozart. Engraved by Thomson after print of Kohl. 1793.

STEWART, Sir ROBT.—Photograph of Giovanni Sgambati. With seven bars of his symphony in D major, in the Composer's autograph.

DAVIE, Mr. J. H.—Portrait of Joseph Haydn. Engraved by W. Arndt, with autograph signature of composer.
—— Portraits of Thomas Tallis and Wm. Byrd. Heliograph.
—— Engraving (unlabelled).

MARSHALL, Mr. JULIAN.—Saint Cecilia's day celebration ticket, Nov. 23, 1696. Engraving by P. Berchet.
—— Psalm of Thanksgiving, sung by the Children at Christ's Hospital. 1641.
—— Ticket of Elizabeth Miller. 18th century.
—— Shop ticket of Davis (Inventor of Improved Pianoforte). 1813.
—— Ticket for the benefit of Signora Schindlerin, by Albanesi, after Rabecca.

GRAPHIC, PROPRIETORS OF THE.—Sir Julius Benedict, drawn from life, by T. Blake Wirgman.

MARSHALL, Mr. JULIAN.—Portrait of Gouter, with a Lute, etched by Lievens.
—— Portrait of Tamburini, by Lane, after Chalon.
—— Caricature Portrait of Tamburini.
—— Autograph letter of Tamburini.

.—MS. of Beethoven. MS. of L. Spohr.

.—Concert de Musique. Engraving.

MARSHALL, Mr. JULIAN.—Autograph Letter of Schumann. 1841.
—— Original Manuscripts, by Robert and Clara Schumann.

COURTAULD, Mr. SYDNEY.—Letter from L. Van Beethoven to Holty.

MARSHALL, Mr. JULIAN.—Portrait of Willoughby, Earl of Abingdon, with his Music-Master, Abel, by Beneditti after Rigaud. 1800. Original manuscript by Rode.

—— Portrait of Rode (Composer). Drawing.
——   „   „   by Riedel. 1813.

MARSHALL, Mr. JULIAN.—Portrait of Philidor (Composer), by Bartolozzi. 1777.

—— Autograph Letter from Philidor to Bartolozzi. 1790.

—— Ticket signed by Philidor.

MUSIC, Royal College of.—Mendelssohn Bartholdy Felix. Autograph Letter to the Sacred Harmonic Society.

MARSHALL, Mr. JULIAN.—Portrait of Richter (Composer), by Guérin. 1785.

—— Portrait of J. G. Albrechtsberger, by Reidel. 1803.

ROSENTHAL'S ANTIQUARIAT, Munich.—Typus Musicæ, der Jugent zur lernung der Musica an Tag geben (Nürnberg). 1598.

MARSHALL, Mr. JULIAN.—Portrait of Gounod.

—— Original Manuscript, by Gounod (Song). 1851.

—— Portraits of Purcell (various).

—— Original Manuscript, by Purcell (Song).

MAITLAND, Mr. J. A. FULLER.—Purcell, after Clostermann. Engraved by Zobel.

MARSHALL, Mr. JULIAN.—Portrait of Weber, by Limbird. 1826.

—— Portrait of Weber, in three positions, by Hayter.

—— Portrait of Schubert (composer), by Kriehuber. 1846.

—— Original Manuscript, by Schubert (Song). 1827.

MOSCHELES, Miss CHARLOTTE.—Mendelssohn's Study. As it was at his death. By Felix Moscheles.

MARSHALL, Mr. JULIAN.—Portrait of Handel, by Houbraken.

—— Original Manuscript, by Beethoven.

—— Autograph letter of Beethoven.

MOSCHELES, Miss CHARLOTTE.—Ignaz Moscheles' Study, by Felix Moscheles.

WILSON, Mr. A.—Portrait of Dr. Croft, engraved by T. Hedgetts, after J. J. Halls.

PICTURES, ETC.

WILLETT, Mr. H.—141. A Guitar Player, by Vanloo.

BROWN, Mr. J. J.—142. The Rival Musicians, by J. Benlliure.

BROADWOOD & SONS, Messrs.—143. Portrait of J. B. Cramer, by J. C. Horsley, R.A.

ABRAHAM, Mr. J.—144. Piece of Tapestry, "Orpheus,' Italian. 16th century.

LITTLETON, Mr. H.—145. Portrait of Sir Michael Costa, by Rosenthal.

JACKSON, Mr. R.—146. Sketches of Military Musical Instruments, engraved by Corré. 1782.

PARSONS, Mr. E.—147. Painting of a Group of Musical Instruments, by Francesco Graldisi.

SOLDATI, Mr.—148. Painting of a Group of Musical Instruments.

—— 149. Painting of a Group of Musical Instruments.

GRAPHIC, PROPRIETORS OF THE.—150. Water-colour Drawing of a Mandoline Player (female).

CHESTER, Mr. JOHN.—151. Water-colour Drawing of a Mandoline Player (male).

DIVISION 26.

On Inner Wall.

NORWOOD, Mr. W.—Portrait of Henry Purcell. Printed for J. Hinton. *n. d.*
—— Portrait of Dr. John Blow. Printed for J. Hinton. *n. d.*

MARSHALL, Mr. JULIAN.—Portrait of Waltz (Handel's Cook, Musician, &c.), by Müller, after Hanck.
—— Autograph Letter of Callcott (on the Musical Scale).
—— Portrait of Callcott.

WILSON, Mr. A.—Portrait of Arcangelo Corelli. Engraved by W. Sherwin.
—— Portraits of Dr. Wm. Boyce. Drawn and engraved by F. K. Sherwin.

MARSHALL, Mr. JULIAN.—Portrait of Handel, by Faber? j
—— Original Manuscript, by Boccherini.
—— Original Manuscript, by Jomelli.
—— Portrait of Jomelli.

BROADWOOD & SONS, Messrs.—Portrait, Carl Maria Von Weber. Taken three days before his death. By Liverati.

PRATTEN, Mrs. S.—Portrait, Mrs. Mountain.

MARSHALL, Mr. JULIAN.—Portrait of Krieger, Composer.
—— The "Concert," by C. Visscher, after Van de Velde.
—— Portrait of Paer, Composer, by Toschi, after Gérard.

.—Portrait.

HILL & SONS, Messrs.—Engraving. The Lute Player.

MARSHALL, Mr. JULIAN.—Portrait of Liszt, by Sir J. Hayter. 1846.
—— Original Manuscript, by Liszt. 1827.
—— Portrait of Spontini, Composer, by Saint Leon.
—— Autograph Letter of Spontini. 1848.
—— Original Manuscript, by Spontini.
—— Portrait of Rubini, by Lane, after Chalon. 1833.

MARSHALL, Mr. JULIAN.—Portrait of Donizetti (caricature).
—— „ Donizetti.
—— Manuscript list of properties required by Donizetti in his Opera " Lucrezia Borgia."
—— A Sunday Concert, 1782, containing Portrait of Pacchierotti.
—— Portrait of Geminiani, by Buchardon.
—— Receipt, signed by Geminiani, June 15, 1751.
—— Portraits of Paer (Drawings).
—— Original Manuscript, by Paer.
—— Portrait of John Hebden.
—— Portrait.
—— Portrait of Ariosti, by Simon. 1719.
—— Title of the Opera " Coliorlano," by Ariosti.
—— Portrait of Piccinni (composer), by Cathelin, after Robineau.
—— Autograph Letter, by Piccini.
—— Original Manuscript, by Piccini.

HORNER, Mr. B.—Portrait of Dr. T. A. Arne. Pencil Drawing.
—— Portrait of Thos. Britton, the Musical Small-coal Man.

MARSHALL, Mr. JULIAN.—Caricature Portrait of Rossini.
—— Portrait of Rossini, by Masson.
—— Document, signed by Rossini. 1840.
—— Autograph Letter of Rossini. 1859.
—— Original Manuscript by Rossini.

CHESTER, Mr. JOHN.—Portrait, Miss Mary Lillias Scott. Engraved by J. Faber.

FORT, Mr. C. H. K..—Portrait, Adolph Hesse. Engraved by A. Herzing. 1862.

DIVISION 27.

LAWRENCE, Mr. A. M.—*Pianoforte*, Spinet shape, by Crang Hancock. 1779.

BROADWOOD & SONS, Messrs. — *Square Piano*, by John Broadwood, London. 1780.

TAPHOUSE, Mr. T. W.—*Square Piano*, by John Broadwood & Son, London. 1795.

PICTURES, &C.

Inner Wall.

LOWENSTEIN, Mr. L.—The "Siesta." After Alma-Tadema, R.A., etched by the Lender.

THE FINE ART SOCIETY.—"The Music Lesson," after Sir F. Leighton, P.R.A.

LEFEVRE, Mr. L. H.—The Vintage Festival, engraved by Auguste Blanchard, after L. Alma Tadema, R.A.

EDWARDS, Mrs.—Lithographs by Fantin. Wagner's "Rheingold" and "Tannhäuser," Brahm's "Rinaldo"—and "Solitude," Schumann.

CRANE, Mr. WALTER.—Drawings, by W. Crane. Pans Pipes.

LEHMANN, Mr. R.—Portraits in black and white of Verdi, 1884; Liszt, 1849; Meyerbeer, 1860; Clara Schumann, 1860; Hiller, 1850; Moscheles, 1850; Joachim, 1851.

Outer Wall.

CONVENT STUDIO, Woodside, Croydon.—151a. Painting on China, St. Cecilia.
—— 152. Frame containing four Paintings on China, illustrating the nursery rhyme of "Tom the Piper's Son."

HORNER, Mr. B.—152a. Portrait of Michael Kelly.

Dowdeswell & Dowdeswell.—153. Seven Photogravures:
(*a*) "Vibrato;" (*b*) "A very difficult passage;"
(*c*) "What will you have?" (*d*) "A Favourite
Morceau;" (*e*) "A sweet strain;" (*f*) "The Dancing-
Master's pay day;" (*g*) "A difficult Passage."

On Partition.

Arkwright, Mr. J. H.—154. Drawing of Westminster
Abbey at the time of the King (George III) and Queen
entering the Royal Gallery on the first day of the com-
memoration of Handel, 26th May, 1784. Drawn by
Colonel Bülow, Foot Guards, and presented by him
to H.R.H. the Princess Augusta, July, 1790.

Doulton, Mr. J.—155. Terra Cotta Panel, "Herodius de-
manding the Head of John the Baptist," by George
Tinworth.

Hallé, Miss Elinor.—156. Plaster Panel, St. Cecilia, by
the Lender.

MUSICAL INSTRUMENTS IN THE HISTORIC ROOMS.

The three rooms fitted in the styles of different periods have been arranged by Mr. GEORGE DONALDSON. The greater part of the furniture, panelling, and other fittings, is lent for the English 18th century Room by Messrs. WRIGHT & MANSFIELD, for the Sixteenth-Century Tudor Room by Mr. GEORGE DONALDSON; and for the French Louis Seize Room by Mr. EDWARD JOSEPHS.

Sixteenth-Century Room.

GRESLEY, Rev. NIGEL, and his brothers.—*Virginal*, known as Queen Elizabeth's Virginal. Italian. 16th century.

DONALDSON, Mr. GEORGE.—*Lectern*, carved oak. Italian. 16th century.
—— *Lute*, Italian, by Tieffenbrucker.
—— *Cetera*, Italian. 16th century.
—— *Arch Lute*, Italian. 16th century.
—— *Coffer*, wood, carved with a frieze of musical subjects, &c. Italian. 16th century.
—— *Horn*, ivory, carved with figures in relief. Danish (?)

SOLDATO, Mr.—*Lute*, Italian. 16th century.

SALAMAN, Mr.—*Harp Lute*, Venetian. 16th century.

English Room, 18th century.

TAPHOUSE, Mr. T. W.—*Quartet Music Desk*, inlaid with representations of musical instruments.

DONALDSON, Mr. GEORGE.—*Oboe*, English. 18th century. By Milhouse, Newark.

PEINIGER, Herr.—*Viola d'Amore*, German. By Johannes Blasius Weigert in Linz. 1723.
—— *Viola da Gamba*, German. About 1700.
—— *Chitarrone*, Venetian. By Michael Atton. 1610.

VALDRIGHI, Count.—*Violoncello.*

CHESTER, Mr. JOHN.—*Cither*, English. 18th century. By Preston.

GOSS, Mr. C. W.—*Harp Lute*, English. 18th century.

DALE, Mr. WILLIAM.—*Spinet*, English. By John Hitchcock. No. 1630.

WILLETT, Mr. HENRY.—Collection of Old English pottery figures, relating to music.

SMITH, Mr. SODEN.—Collection of Old Silver in corner cupboard.

Salon, Louis XVI.

POWERSCOURT, Viscount.—*Clavecin* or *Harpsichord*, by Hans Ruckers of Antwerp. Double keyboard. Dated 1612. Restored by Taskin, 1774. Painted with scenes of the period of Louis XIV. by Van der Meulen. Said to have belonged to Marie Antoinette.

JOSEPHS, Mr. EDWARD.—*Harp*, French. Belonged to George IV.
—— *Mandoline*, French.
—— *Small Music Desk*, wood, inlaid with representations of musical instruments.
—— *Bagpipes*, French.
—— *Harp Lute.*
—— *Music Desk*, wood, open-worked.
—— Collection of *Miniature Musical Instruments*, in cabinet.
—— *Cither*, inlaid with silver and pearl.
—— *Guitar*, inlaid with pearl. Perforated sides.

COLEMAN, Mr. C. CARYL.—*Lute*, ivory. Venetian. By Jacob Hesin. 1586.

DONALDSON, Mr. GEORGE.—*Lute Case*, stamped leather. French. 18th century.

DIVISION 28.

On Inner Wall.

MARSHALL, Mr. JULIAN.—Portrait of Senesino, by Van-
haecken, after Hudson. 1735.
—— Portrait of Miss Stephens, by Say, after Harlow. 1816.

.—Portrait

MARSHALL, Mr. JULIAN.—Portrait of Mrs. Robinson, by Faber,
after Vanderbank.
—— Portrait of Leveridge, by Van der Mijn.
——   „   John Broadwood, by W. Say, after Harrison.
——   „   Lindley (Violoncellist), by Quilley, after
Davison.

.—Portrait of Cosimo (violinist), by Smith,
after Kneller.

ORIENTAL ROOM.

ORIENTAL INSTRUMENTS.

Centre of Room.

MUSIC, Royal College of.—*Musical Box*, playing Indian airs.

FERRARI, Miss.—*Seraphine*, by Fourneaux

Glass Case.

.—Book of Javese Music and Plates of Musical Instruments, by Sir Stamford Raffles.

H.M. THE QUEEN.—*Flageolet.*
—— *Part of a Gambang.*
—— *Four Zournas* (Hindustan).
—— *Percussion Instrument.*
—— *Algooza.*
—— *War Trumpet* of Ashantee.

MUSIC, Royal College of.—Models of Javese musical instruments, in silver filagree.

WARRINGTON, Corporation of.—*Cane Musical Instrument,* with resonance gourd. West Africa.

STONYHURST, The Very Rev. the Rector of.—*Persian Handbell.*
—— *Pair of Cymbals.* Persian.

OAKELEY, Sir HERBERT.—*Flute.* Japanese.
—— *Two Sonas,* Chinese.
—— *Rebec,* Three Strings.
—— *Indian Trumpet.*
—— *Tai Hoo* (Chinese Trumpet.)
—— *Indian Pipe,* carved mouth.
—— *Indian Pipe,* eight holes; curious reed.

I

SIEVEKING, Mr. E. H.—*Syrinx*. Admiralty Islands.

RIVINGTON, Rev. J. A.—*Drum*. Moorish.

SOUTH, Mrs. W. A.—*Drum*. Moorish.

VEITCH & SONS, Messrs.—*Syrinx*, or *Mouth Organ*.

————

VERNEY, Sir HARRY, Bart., M.P.—*Collection of Javese Instruments*, formerly belonging to Sir Stamford Raffles.
—— *Two Kettle-shaped Gongs*, with boss to strike upon.
—— *Seven Gambang Sáron* (7 bars).
—— *Metal Gambang*, with pipe resonators.
—— *Two large Gongs*, suspended in a frame painted and richly gilt.
—— *Metal Gambang* (11 bars), on a deep frame with carved idol.
—— *Gambang Kajoe*, wood, 20 bars.
—— *Small Gambang*, wood, 17 bars.
—— *Large Gambang*, wood, 18 bars.
—— *Javese Drum*.

MUSIC, Royal College of.—*Kheradak* and *Khoradak*.

The two instruments are played upon, both at the same time, with the fingers and palms of the two hands. The one played upon with the right hand gives a sharp sound—and the one with the left produces the deep sound. These instruments are played in the Rawoshunchawki.

—— *Jagajhampa*. Formerly used on warlike, but now on festive occasions.
—— *Dhak*.

Formerly known as the Dhakká, and used in the war field, but now the instrument is used on occasions of religious festivities, such as the Durgá Pújá, Charaka Pújá, &c. The right hand side of the instrument is played upon with two sticks, the left hand side is not played at all.

—— *Tikara* and *Bom*. Played together, each with a stick.
—— *Joraghayi*.

This is a double instrument; one dhola being played upon another of a larger size. The right side is played upon with a stick; the left with the hand.

—— *Tasa*. Formerly used on warlike, but now on festive occasions.
—— *Mridanga*.

An ancient instrument, said to have been invented by the Hindu deity Brahmá. The Mridanga is intended to accompany classical forms of songs and hymns. It is sometimes played with the Mahati Viná, Rudra Viná, &c.

MUSIC, Royal College of.—*Marddala.*

Commonly known as the Mádala. The Marddala is chiefly used by the aboriginal tribes, such as the Bhíls, Kols. Sanchéls, &c., of Birbhum, Midnapus, Senri, and other hilly places in the Province of Bengal. This instrument is a classical one, being, evidently, a corrupted form of the Mridanga.

—— *Dholaka.*

This instrument is generally used to accompany songs sung in Játtrá, Pánchéli, Half-Akrái, and other semi-operatic performances.

—— *Bányá* and *Tablá.*

The Bányá is played upon with the left hand, and the Tablá (sometimes called the Dáhiná) with the right. This pair is a modern invention; the idea being taken from the Mridanga, the left end of which is represented by the Bányá, and the right end by the Tablá.

—— *Panaba.* A small drum or tabor; a very classical instrument.

MAHILLON & Co., Messrs.—*Khoradak.* Played with fingers and palms of the hand.

—— *Banya.* Played in conjunction with the Tabla, in the left hand.

—— *Fekara.* Played in conjunction with the Damama, each with one stick.

—— *Dagara.* Played in conjunction with Jhuridhap, each with one stick.

—— *Kara.* Used formerly in times of war, now on festive occasions.

—— *Damama.* Played in conjunction with Fikara, each with one stick.

—— *Jhuridhap.* Played in conjunction with Dagara, each with one stick.

—— *Fasa.* Used on festive occasions.

—— *Jagajhampa.* Used on festive occasions.

—— *Mridanga.* Invented by Hindoo God Brahma. Used for accompaniment in solemn music and hymns.

—— *Nyastaranga.*

This instrument has the appearance of a wind instrument, but is never blown. A portion of a spider's web is placed on the part of the instrument which looks like the mouthpiece. It is then placed on the throat, upon the vocal chords, and, being breathed upon hardly, produces a clear ready note. It is said that a sound can also be produced by placing the instrument upon the cheeks and the nostrils.

—— *Khoradak.* Played with fingers and palms of the hand.

—— *Murddhala.* Used by aboriginal tribes in hilly places.

—— *Joraghayi.* Double instrument. The right side is played with a stick, the left with the hand.

I 2

MAHILLON & Co., Messrs.—*Panaba*. Small drum ; classical instrument.

—— *Tabla*. Played in conjunction with the Banya, in the right hand.

On or near the Walls.

VEITCH & SONS, Messrs.—*Reed Flute*. South Sea Islands.

—— *Tamboura Baghlama* (Turkish), said to have come from South America.

—— *Two Cruries*.

SOUTH, Mrs. W. A.—*Balafong*, African.

—— *Sanko*, African.

PEINIGER, HERR—*Crurie*, Borneo (7 pipes in calabash).

—— *Urheen and bow*, Chinese.

—— *Darbouka* (Algiers), kind of guitar.

—— ,, ,,

—— *Sarinda*, Hindoo.

—— *Chikarah*, Indian.

—— *Zulu Stringed Instrument*, with gourd.

YOUNG, Mr. W.—*Indian Free-reed Instrument*, resembling the Chinese Cheng.

WYBARD, Mr. F. J.—*Tamboura*.

—— *Sanko*. Ashantee.

.—*Tamboura*.

RIVINGTON, Rev. J. A.—*Gusla* (Montenegrin Fiddle).

GUINNESS, Miss M.—*Native Instrument*, African.

OAKELEY, Sir. H.—*Thro*. Burmese Finger-board inlaid with pearl.

MUSIC, Royal College of.—*Two Baratakas*. Wind instruments used in religious services.

H.M. THE QUEEN—*Pair of Cymbals*.

—— *Pair of Cymbals*. Brass. Indian.

—— ,, ,, ,, Chinese.

—— *Small Drum*. Asiatic wood and skin, fringed with hair.

—— *Drum*. Chinese. Wood, with skin top.

—— *Rattle*, used by Chinese beggars.

—— *Shell Instrument*. South Sea.

—— *Percussion Instrument* (military). German.

—— *Pair of small Bells*.

—— *Native Drum*. New Britain Island.

—— *Pipa Tambourine*, Chinese.

OAKELEY, Sir HERBERT.—*Two Yue-Kin,* or *Moon Guitars,* Chinese.
—— *Two Pipas,* Chinese.

STONYHURST COLLEGE.—*Pair of Persian Cymbals.*
—— *Trumpet,* made by the natives, from the tusk of an African elephant.

JAPANESE FINE ART ASSOCIATION.—*Old Miniature Koto,* 13 strings, of Coromandel wood, ivory mounted.
—— *Japanese Koto,* 13 strings. Coromandel wood, to represent the effect of tortoise shell.

VEITCH & SONS, Messrs.—*Ty,* or *Chinese Flute.*

OAKELEY, Sir HERBERT.—*Cheng.* Chinese mouth organ. 17 pipes.
—— Three " *Tay Woocum.*" Chinese.
—— " *Ee Woocum.*" Chinese.
—— Three *Wang Tieng.* Chinese flutes.
—— 2 *Stands for Chinese Drums.*
—— *Yang-chin,* or *Dulcimer.* Chinese.
—— *San-heen.* (Pekin Band, J. H. E., *Sien tzê*).
—— *Yong-koo* (Chinese drum).
—— *Tom-tom.*
—— *Drum,* wooden, painted. Indian.
——   „   earthenware, painted. Indian.

H.M. THE QUEEN. — *San-heen,* usual snake-skin top and bottom, Chinese.
—— *Sixteen stringed Instrument,* Indian. Resembling the Chinese Kin.

ALLEN, Mr. G.—*Ur-heen,* Chinese.

SOUTH, Mrs. W. A.—*Tamboura.*

RIVINGTON, Rev. J. A.—*Tamboura,* Moorish.

HIPKINS, Miss EDITH.—*Water colour of a Japanese Koto Player,* by the lender.

H.M. THE QUEEN.—*Tom-tom.*
—— *Drum,* probably Chinese.
—— *Tamboura Fiddle.* Chinese.
—— *Drum,* carved from a tree trunk, perforated by musket shots. Two human jaws attached to it. The war drum of the King of Ashantee.
—— *Tom-tom,* copper and parchment, with silk fringe.
—— Indian instrument with three strings.

H.M. THE QUEEN.—Two *Rattle Tom-toms*, Chinese.
—— *Talain Vrgee Wain and Stand.* Buddhist.
—— *Guitar*, made from the head of the Duke of Schom-
berg's horse, killed at the Battle of the Boyne, 1690.
—— Two *Sarindas*, inlaid with ivory, Indian.
—— *Megyoung*, six strings, Burmese. In the form of an
alligator.

HARFORD, Rev. Canon.—*Sitár*, Indian.

CHESTER, Mr. JOHN—*Sitár*, body formed of a gourd, Indian.

PEINIGER, Herr.—*Yue-kin* or *Moon guitar.*

KENNEDY, Mr. E. H.—*Sitár*, Indian.

MAHILLON & Co., Messrs.—*Kattyauna Viná*, now called
Kanoon, formerly called Shata Tantri Viná, or the hundred wired Viná.

STONYHURST COLLEGE. — *Malagasy Musical Instrument*,
brought from Nosvery by F. Perry and presented to
Stonyhurst Museum. The strings are cut out and raised
from the fibres of the wood.

H.M. THE QUEEN.—Three *Pairs of Cymbals.* Brass.

.—*Burmese Harp.*

VEITCH & SONS, Messrs.—*Borneo Instrument.*
—— *Malagasy Musical Instrument.*

PICTURES, &c.

MAHILLON & Co., Messrs.—Photograph representing the
private band of Rajah Sourindro Mohun Tagore.

—— Water colour. Religious ceremony on the banks of the
Ganges.

—— Six oil paintings, representing Hindoo musicians.

———

MAHILLON & Co, Messrs.—*Sankha.* Conch trumpet used in
Buddhist temples.
—— *Gemakha.* Conch trumpet, somewhat like the mouth
of a cow, whence its name.
—— *Anantu Vizaya.* Conch used by Rajah Yudhisthira in
Kurukshetha war.

MAHILLON & Co., Messrs.—*Sughosa.* Conch said to have been used by Nacub, the brother of Rajah Yudhisthira.

—— *Rana Stringa.* Formerly used in military bands, now in religious processions.

—— *Barutuka.* Large conch trumpet.

—— *Furi.* Indian trumpet, used on occasions of war and in the Nahabat.

—— *Stringa.* Indian horn, favourite instrument of the Hindu God Siva.

—— *Murali.* Indian flute, invented by Hindu God Khrishna.

—— *Garala Bansi.* Indian flageolet.

—— *Dara.* Large size Khanyani.

—— *Kalama.* So called from its likeness to a pen (kalama).

—— *Mandira.* Two cups used to keep the measure of the time in a musical performance.

—— *Kudra Ghunta.* Little bells used to keep time.

—— *Khattuli.* Hindu castinets.

—— *Laya Bansi.* Blown like the Arabian Nay from one of the ends.

—— *Haruk.* Large-sized damaru.

—— *Maha Mandira.* Large-sized mandira.

—— *Shanaye.* Played in the Nahabat or Indian Brass Band on festive occasions and weddings, generally on top of gates or triumphal arches.

—— *Kausara.* Played with a stick, used in temples at the time of worship.

—— *Fubri.* Used by snake-charmers.

—— *Ghuri.* Indian gong.

—— *Thanaye.* Played in the Nahabat or Indian Brass Band.

—— *Mochango.* Similar to the English Jews' harp.

—— *Nyastaranga.* Played with a spider's web, which is placed over the mouthpiece.

—— *Ghangh Khanjani.* Supplied with two small cymbals.

—— *Ghaghara.* Set of little bells worn at the ankle of dancers to keep time.

—— *Kharatala.* Cymbals as used in the Nahabat.

—— *Ghungura.* Set of little bells worn at the ankle by dancers to keep time.

—— *Khanjani.* Used by religious mendicants.

—— *Kausi.* Played with a stick, keeps time with the dhola.

—— *Naphura.* Used like the ghungura and ghaghara.

—— *Kuratala.* Cymbals used with the khol.

MAHILLON & Co., Messrs.—*Dindimi.* Small sized khanyani.

—— *Ghauta.* Bell used at the time of worship.

—— *Damaru.* Used by snake-charmers and monkey-players.

Benu. Classical instrument, used in Orissa.

—— *Ranjani Viná.* Two gourds, like Mahati Viná.

—— *Chikara.* Strings made of horsehair.

—— *Fumburu Viná.* Used in vocal and instrumental performances, and by continuing the sound saves pauses.

—— *Kinnari Viná.* Modified form of Kacchapi Viná.

—— *Sar Bahara.* Specially adapted for playing Alapas of Ragas and Raginis.

—— *Sarangi.* Used in performances of Indian Nautch girls.

—— *Kacchapi Viná.* So called from the shape of the gourd, flat, like the back of the tortoise.

—— *Fritanki Viná* (generally called Setar).

—— *Sar Viná.* Something like the Rudra Viná, but it is played with a bow.

—— *Pinaka.* Invention of the God Siva, and said to be the father of all stringed instruments.

—— *Sursanga.* Formed of the Esrar and the Setár.

—— *Esrar.* For accompaniment of female voices.

—— *Khudra Kattyanna Vina.* Kattyanna Viná in smaller size.

—— *Rudra Viná.* Known as Rabab; used in Persia.

—— *Sur Stringara.* Composition of Mahati Kacchapi and Rudra Vina.

—— *Sarinda.* Ancient instrument, rough shape of the Sarangi.

—— *Alabu Sarangi.* Indian Violin.

—— *Ananda Sahari.* Mostly used by beggars.

—— *Shuradiya Viná.* Known as Sharode, used in Upper Provinces of India.

—— *Bipanchi Viná.* Hollow, made of gourd, known in Bengal as the Fith Lavo.

—— *Nadesvara Viná.* A modern instrument.

—— *Kasta Viná.* A modern instrument.

—— *Shank-Ktika Viná.* Hollow, of mother-o'-pearl.

—— *Bhorata Viná.* A modern instrument.

—— *Sarjogi.* Modified form of Sarangi.

—— *Fausar Mayuri.* Derives name from figure of peacock (Mayuri).

—— *Ektara.* Used by religious mendicants for accompaniment to their songs.

—— *Mina Sarangi.* Derives name from figure of a fish (mina).

MAHILLON & Co., Messrs.—*Prasarina Viná.* A Tritraniti Viná, with double finger board.

——— *Kinnari Viná.* Presentation instrument.

——— *Sruti Viná.* This shows the 22 sruties which exist in an octave.

——— *Gopijantra.* Used by religious mendicants for accompaniment in their songs.

——— *Fumbura Viná.* Presentation instrument.

——— *Kairata Viná.* One gourd only and 6 frets.

——— *Mahati Viná.* Ancient instrument, invented by Page Marada.

H.M. THE QUEEN. — *Brass Gong.* Taken from Tippoo Sahib's tent.

On the Floor.

MAHILLON & Co., Messrs.—*Dholaka.* Used in outdoor music.

——— *Dhola.* Used on festive occasions.

——— *Ghutru.* Used by the Telegues tribes.

——— *Dhak.* Right side played with two sticks, left side left out altogether.

MUSIC, ROYAL COLLEGE OF.—*Dampha.* For accompaniment in prayers.

——— *Khol.* For accompaniment in religious songs.

H.M. THE QUEEN.—*Drum.* Bronze-chased. Siamese.

On the Walls.

MUSIC, Royal College of.—*The Ranjani-Viná.*

It has, like the Mahati Viná, two gourds attached to the ends, but is played upon and tuned exactly like the Kachchhapi.

——— *The Tumburu-Viná,* better known as Tumburu.

The invention of this instrument is attributed to the Celestial musician, Tumburu. The instrument is intended to accompany vocal or instrumental performances, and is the indicator of the keynote adopted.

——— *Benu.*

The Benu is a popular instrument with the people of Orissa. A classical instrument, about four feet six inches in length, and made of bamboo wood.

——— *Shauktika-Viná.*

The hollow of this instrument is made of mother-of-pearl. In every other respect it is just like the Kachchhapi.

——— *Pinaka.*

The instrument is known to have been the invention of the Hindu God, Síva, and is said to be the father of stringed instruments.

Music, Royal College of.—*Prasarani-Viná.*

The instrument is a Tritantri-Vina, with two finger-boards (a modern invention).

—— *Sarinda.*

A rude form of the Sarangi, and known to be an ancient instrument, now generally used by the classes of Durwán's (gatekeepers, &c.).

—— *Sruti-Viná.*

An ancient instrument of the Setár class, showing the twenty-two Srutis or enharmonic intervals which exist in an octave.

—— *Gopiyantra,* used exclusively by Vairágis and Bául's [religious mendicants] for accompanying pastoral songs.

The instrument is mounted with one string, the different sounds being produced by the compressions or otherwise of the fingers, with which the lower part of the instrument is held.

—— *Sursanga.*

The instrument is formed out of the Esrár and Setár. In fact, it is nothing but the Esrár without the side wires. The first instrument of this kind is said to have been made by Sebaram Dass, of Vishnupur (an ancient city of Bengal).

H.M. The Queen.—*Brass Trumpet.*
—— *Gong.* Chinese.

Music, Royal College of.—*Mina Sarangi.*

Another form of the Esrar. With the exception of the finger-board, the whole instrument is made of one entire piece of gourd. The instrument derives its name from the figure of a fish (Mina), which is attached to the end of the hollow.

—— *Bipancha-Viná.* The hollow of this instrument is made of a peculiar kind of gourd known in Bengal as the Tith Láu.

—— *Alabu Sarangi.* Called by some European writers on Hindoo Music the Indian Violin.

The surface of this instrument is like that of the violin, having a gourd hollow under it. This instrument is known to be a very old one.

—— *Ananda-Lahari.* An instrument mostly used by singing beggars.

It consists of one catgut, the variety of sounds produced by which is due to the different degrees of tension to which it is subjected.

—— *Rudra Viná.*

The instrument is known at present as "Rabab," and in Arabia as "Rubeb." It is extensively used in Persia, Afghanistan, and the North-Western Provinces of India; also in Siam and Java.

—— *Sur-Sringara.* The instrument is a combination of the Mahati, Kachchhapi, and Rudra Viná, devised by the celebrated Viná player, Piyár Khan.

MUSIC, Royal College of.—*Kairata Viná*. The instrument has one gourd and six frets. It looks partially like the Mahati-Viná.

—— *Saradiya Viná*.

The "Sarod," by which name the instrument is known at present, is mostly used in the Upper Provinces. It was formerly used as an out-door instrument in royal processions.

—— *Sarangi*. A very sweet toned ancient instrument, intended to accompany the female voice.

The instrument is generally used in the performances of the Hindustani Nautch girls.

—— *Chikara*. The instrument is generally used by Durwans, Syces (grooms), &c., &c. The strings of the instrument are all made of horsehair.

—— *Bharata-Viná*. A modern instrument formed out of the Rudra and Kachchhapi-Viná.

—— *Tritantri Viná*.

Also an ancient instrument, now going by the general name of "Setar" (or three wires), given to it by Amir Khusru, in the 13th century. The hollow of this instrument is sometimes made of wood. In other respects the instrument is just like the Kachchhapi. Originally it had three wires.

—— *Nadesvera-Viná*. A very modern instrument, formed out of the violin and Kachchhapi-Viná.

—— *Taus* or *Mayuri*. A form of the Esrar.

The instrument derives its name from the figure of a peacock (Mayúr) which is attached to the end of the hollow.

—— *Kachchhapi-Viná*. A classical instrument, known at present as Kachua Setár.

The instrument owes its name to the shape of the gourd, which is flat, like the back of a tortoise (Kachhapa).

—— *Ektara*. Used exclusively by Vairágis and Bauls [religious mendicants] for accompanying pastoral songs.

The instrument is mounted with one string.

—— *Sur-Viná*. A classical instrument, somewhat resembling the Rudra-Viná in appearance.

—— *Sanyogi*. A modified form of the Sarangi, a modern invention.

—— *Sur Bahara*.

A large-sized Kachchhapi-Viná, invented about sixty years ago by Golam Mahomed, Khan of Lucknow. It is especially adapted for the playing of Alapas of Rágas and Ráginis.

H.M. THE QUEEN.—*Halbmond*, German bugle-horn.

—— *Drum*.

MUSIC, Royal College of.—*Mahati-Viná*.

A very ancient instrument, said to have been invented by the Sage Nárada. It is the best and the most difficult of all Hindu musical instruments.

—— *Ghanta*.

A ringing bell used at the time of worship.

—— *Turi*.

The Indian trumpet used on occasions of war, also with the Nahabat.

—— *Thanjh-Khanjani*.

The instrument is supplied with two small cymbals, which make a jingling sound when it is struck upon.

—— *Ghaghara*. A set of jingles, a variety of the Ghungura.

—— *Rana-Sringa*.

An instrument formerly used in military bands. It is now used in religious processions.

—— *Din dimi*, a smaller variety of the Khanjani.

—— *Sankha*.

A very ancient instrument, formerly used on warlike, religious and festive occasions, now only on the latter, this instrument might not inappropriately be called the father of wind instruments in days of yore. Sankhas of various descriptions were in use, such as the Pancha Janya (used by Krishna), Devadatta (used by Arjjuna, &c.). The Sankha is also used in the Buddhist temples, the instrument is sometimes called by Europeans the conch trumpet.

—— *Khanjani*.

A tabor-like instrument, used by religious mendicants and pastoral singers.

—— *Ghungura*.

A set of jingles or little bells, worn at the ankles by dancers to keep time to the dancing.

—— *Mandira*.

The sound of this instrument is produced by two cups of bell metal striking against each other. The Mandira is used to measure out the time in a musical performance.

—— *Mochanga*.

A very ancient instrument. It has to be held against the teeth by means of the left hand, and the wire to be gently tapped with the forefinger of the right hand. The instrument gives only one note.

—— *Napura*, used like the Ghungura and Ghaghara for dancing purposes.

—— *Ghari*.

The Indian gong played upon with a stick. An instrument of very great vibration.

—— *Shánáyi*, as played in the Nahabat.

The Shánáyi calla Sharna in Persia, is said to have been a favourite instrument with the Mogul Emperor Akbar Shah.

Music, Royal College of.—*Huruk,* a large sized Damaru used by the Kaharas and other lower tribes.

—— *Tubri,* called Tiktiri in Sanskrit.

A rude instrument used by snake-charmers.

—— *Sarala Bansi.* The Indian flageolet.

The instrument has to be held straight before the mouth when played upon.

—— *Karatala.* Cymbals accompanying the Khob.
—— *Dara.* A larger variety of the Khanjani.
—— *Laya Bansi.*

Like the Sarala Bansi the instrument has to be held straight before the mouth, but it has to be blown into from one extremity of the lips.

—— *Nyastaranga.*

A trumpet-shaped instrument, has to be placed upon the vocal chords, sounds from which produce by vibration a clear reedy note upon the instrument; it is believed that an instrument of this description is scarcely to be met with in any other part of the world than India; it is known in Sanskrit as the Upánga, and is extensively used by Hindoos in the North Western Provinces, and particularly at Mathúra and Brindaban.

—— *Kalama.* So called because of its likeness to the pen [Kalama].
—— *Shanayi.* As used by the people of Orissa.
—— *Kansara.* A small gong used in temples and other religious places at the time of worship.
—— *Bansi.* The Indian flute made of bamboo wood. The invention of the instrument is ascribed to the Hindu Deity Krishna, who is described to have been very fond of it.
—— *Khattali.* The castanets of the Hindus.

The instrument consists of two steel bars.

—— *Sringa.* The Indian horn.

The instrument is said to have been a favourite of the Hindu Deity, Siva.

—— *Damaru.*

A very ancient instrument, said to have been the favourite of the Hindu, Siva. The Damaru is now generally used by snake charmers and monkey players.

H.M. The Queen.—*Sang.* (Boat-shaped harp.) Burmese.

.—*Kip,* Chinese.
—— *Burmese Harp.*
—— *Rana Sringa.*

On the Floor.

Music, Royal College of.—*Khol.*

Pulsatile instrument covered with skin; chiefly used to accompany the Kirtana and other religious songs.

—— *Dampha.*

A pulsatile instrument covered with skin (used in religious service), used by the Vaisagis and other religious mendicants. The instrument is chiefly meant to accompany Bhajan or prayer songs.

—— *Ghutru.*

Also a pulsatile instrument (pastoral). It is used by the Telegoos and other people of the Madras Presidency.

—— *Dhol.*

A pulsatile instrument (pastoral), as used by the people of Orissa. The instrument looks something like the Dhák.

THE special exhibition of musical instruments lent by His
Majesty the King of Siam, and shown under the tent in the
East Central Gallery, adjacent to the Music Room, having
arrived too late to find place in the Second Edition of the
Official Catalogue, is here mentioned. It completes the
Ethnological Group from India to China. The Siamese
instruments are beautifully made and ornamented with ivory
and mother-of-pearl. They consist of specimens of wooden
harmonicons, the Ranat Ek (treble) and the Ranat Thoom
(bass) ; of metal harmonicons, the Ranat Thong (treble) and
the Ranat Leck (bass). These are analogoes of the Javese
Gambang, but with a peculiar heptatonic scale instead of the
pentatonic scales of Java. The Javese Bonang has been
borrowed by Siam, and is the Khong Yai of large, and Khong
Leck, of small gongs. The bowed Saw Thai (Siamese Fiddle)
is the Javese Rabab; the Saw Chine is borrowed from the
Chinese Ur-heen. The interesting Takhay, or "crocodile,"
is a trichord with bridges, played by a plectrum. These
complete the more important stringed instruments. The
wind are Pee, a kind of Oboe, and Klui, a Flute à bec, with
a large reed mouth-organ called Phan. The percussion are
Tambourines and Drums. The performances of the Siamese
Band have made the tone of these instruments familiar to
visitors of the Exhibition.

INNER ROOM.

ENTRANCE THROUGH ORIENTAL ROOM.

PRYER, Mr. JOHN—*Square Piano*, by Longman & Lukey, with Harp stop.

PYNE, Mr. KENDRICK—Two *Harpsichords*, by J. & A. Kirkman. 1773 and 1789.

HEATHCOTE, The Dowager Lady.—*Harpsichord*, by F. Coston. 18th century. London.

DALE, Mr. — *Harpsichord*, by John Broadwood & Sons. London. 1805.

EXETER, Marquess of.—*Square Piano*, by Longman & Broderip. London.

STRATTON, Mr. S. S.—*Clavichord* (Gebunden), formerly Carl Engel's.

PYNE, Mr. KENDRICK.—*Square Piano*, by Zumpe & Buntebart. 1773.

WILLIAMSON, Mr. G.—*Square Piano*, by Zumpe & Buntebart. 1769. London.

WAGGETT & SON, Messrs.—*Square Piano*, by Zumpe & Buntebart. 1770. London.

POHLMAN & SON, Messrs.—*Square Piano*, by Johannes Pohlman. 1773. London.

BROADWOOD & SONS, Messrs. JOHN.—*Transposing Square Piano*, by the Lenders. Ryley's patent. 1808.
—— *Transposing Cottage Piano*. 1845. The property of Dr. Cornish.

ROGERS, Mr. R. M.—*Clavichord*, by H. W. Langguth, of Breitenbach. 1760.

Collection of eight violins and bows.

KUNST UND GEWERBE MUSEUM, Berlin.—*Spinet.*

KIRKMAN & SONS, Messrs.—*Spinet*, by Player, exhibited 1872.

RUSSELL, Mr. JAMES.—*Spinet*, by Baker Harris. 1763. London.

PYNE, Mr. KENDRICK.—*Spinet*, by Joseph Harris. 1750. London.

PARRATT, Mr. WALTER.—*Spinet*, by Longman & Broderip. London.

PYNE, Mr. KENDRICK.—*Spinet*, by Longman & Broderip. London.

BURGESS, Mr. W.—*Clock*, latter half of 18th century, English.

This clock was made at Maidstone, and contains a barrel-pipe organ that plays thirty-three tunes.

.—Budapest. *Clavicembalo.*

Apparently Venetian. Mother of pearl natural keys and ebony sharps inlaid with ivory. Painted ivory plaques of musicians above the keyboard.

ROOM ON RIGHT OF STAIRCASE FROM CONSERVATORY.

WILLIAMSON, Mr. GEORGE.—*Square Piano,* by Culliford.

TAPHOUSE, Mr. T. W.—*Square Piano,* by Zumpe. 1767.

ALSTON, Mr. T. B.—*Square Piano.* English; "J. Zumpe et Buntebart, Londini, fecerunt, 1770."

HOLDER, Mr. T. W.—*Spinet.* English.

GILBY, Mrs. H. S.—*Lyre-shaped Pianoforte,* with keyboard, by J. C. Schliep.

TAPHOUSE, Mr. G. W.—*Clavichord,* by Joh. Paul Kraemer und Soehnen. Göttingen, 1803, acquired by the late Carl Engel.

CHATTERTON, Mr. JOSEPH.—*Clavichord,* originally a Square Pianoforte, by John Broadwood & Sons. Altered and invented by the Lender.

WILLIAMSON, Mr. G.—*Spinet,* by Thomas Barton. 1719, London.

CRAWFORD, Mr. C.—*Organ.*

KIRKMAN & SONS, Messrs.—*Upright Grand Piano,* by Kirkman. About 1800.
—— *Spinet,* by J. Kirkman. 1755, London.

HODGE & ESSEX, Messrs.—*Piano,* by Graf, of Vienna, made for Beethoven.

This piano was made by Conrad Graf, of Vienna, for Beethoven, during the latter years of that Composer's life. After his death it again passed into the hands of the maker, who sold it to the Wimmer family (Vienna), who recently disposed of it to t e exhibitors. The piano is provided with four chords from D major upwards in order to render it as strong in tone as possible; this was rendered necessary by the fact of Beethoven being deaf during his later years.

POHLMAN & SON, Messrs.—*Square Pianoforte,* by Johannes Pohlman. 1768, London.

SMALLFIELD, Mr. F.—*Harpsichord*, Italian; " Niccolò Berti fece." Repaired, 1864.

HORSLEY, Miss ROSAMOND. — *Spinet*, by John Plenius. London, 1765.

DYSON, Mr.—*Small Square Pianoforte*, by Lenkfeld.

HORSLEY, Mr. J. C., R.A.—*Harpsichord*, by J. Ruckers. 1637, Antwerp.

KIRKMAN & SON, Messrs.—*Harpsichord*, by J. Kirkman. 1752, London.

DALE, Mr. H. J.— *Harpsichord*, " Jacobus et Abraham Kirckman." 1787."

PYNE, Mr. KENDRICK.—*Harpsichord*, by Burkat Shudi and Johannes Broadwood. 1776. No. 789.

LLOYD, Mr. C. H.—*Harpsichord*. English, 1781. " Burkat Shudi et Johannes Broadwood, Londini, fecerunt." No. 902.

STRATTON, Mr. S. S.—*Harpsichord*. English, 1782. " Burkat Shudi et Johannes Broadwood, Londini, fecerunt." No. 919.

TAPHOUSE, Mr. T. W. — *Harpsichord*. English, 1781. " Burkat Shudi et Johannes Broadwood, Londini, fecerunt." No. 899.

DALE, Mr. H. J.—*Double Harpsichord*, by Shudi. 1760, London. With Venetian Swell added about 1770–80. No. 407.

WILSON, Mr. ARTHUR.—*Double Harpsichord*, by J. and A. Kirkman. 1788, London.

BROADWOOD, JOHN, & SONS, Messrs.—*Harpsichord*, by Burkat Shudi. 1771, London. No. 639.

PYNE, Mr. KENDRICK. — *Harpsichord*, by Longman & Broderip.

SIMPSON, Mr. ALEXANDER.—*Upright Square Pianoforte*. Patented by William Southwell, Parish of St. Martin-in-the-fields, about 1798.

INDEX OF LENDERS.

Richardson, Rev. J., 32
Ripon, Dean and Chapter of, 82, 95
Rivington, Rev. J. A., 114, 116, 117
Robertson, W. W., 85
Roche, O., 77
——, Miss C., 61
——, Miss O., 70
——, Miss N., 78
Rockstro, W. S., 68
Rogers, R. M., 128
Rosenthal, L., 67
Rosenthal's Antiquarial, Munich, 68, 83, 85, 88, 89, 92, 95, 104
Rothschild, Baron F. de, 44
Rowland, —, 7
Rudall, Carte & Co., 55, 56
Russell, J., 129

Sacchi, F., 15
St. Gall (Switzerland), Library of, 66
St. Gregory's Monastery, Downside, 84
St. John's College, Cambridge, 68, 96
St. Paul's, Dean and Chapter of, 69, 86, 87
St. Peter's College, Cambridge, 69
Salaman, —, 110
Salisbury, Dean and Chapter of, 96
Samary, G., 43, 44, 45, 53, 57
Sandeman, E. A., 10, 23
Sandys, Lt.-col. T. M., 9, 14
Savenau, Baron von, 90
Scheurleer, D. F., 43, 44, 84, 98
Selle, Dr. W. C., 3, 11, 40
Seilliére, M. le Baron, 14, 32
Selvier, E. de, 44
Siéveking, E. H., 114
Shrewsbury, Bishop of, 84
Shuttleworth, T. M., 22
Simpson, R., 131
Skene, Miss, 56
Smallfield, F., 70, 131
Smart, Miss, 57, 85
Smith, H., 16
——, Rev. H. C., 13
——, R. H. Soden, 111
Snoeck, C., 69, 70
Soldati, —, 105, 110
South, Mrs. W. A., 114, 116, 117
South Kensington Museum, 3
Spencer, Earl, 3, 5, 16, 56, 66, 68, 69, 80, 82, 88, 93
Squire, W. B., 24, 75
Stamp, W., 10
Steuart, C. D., 56
Stewart, Sir R., 51, 58, 71, 103
Stone, Dr. W. H., 58
Stonyhurst, The Very Rev. the Rector of, 58, 95, 113, 117, 118
Strange, H. le, 24

Stratton, S. S., 128, 131
Street, J. E., 3, 50
Suffolk, E., 52
Swears, H., 40
Symes, W. H., 10

Tadema, Mr. Alma, 1
——, Mrs. Alma, 2
Tamplini, G., 55
Taphouse, T., W., 39, 53, 59, 61, 69, 70, 71, 72, 73, 74, 77, 78, 86, 87, 91, 93, 94, 108, 110, 130, 131
Taudou, M., 29
Thewalt, Mons., 58
Tollemache, of Helmingham, Lord, 33
Trinity College, Cambridge, 69, 74, 82
Tyrell, A., 15

University Library, Cambridge, 69, 95, 96

Valdrighi, Count, 43, 49, 52, 59, 111
Van de Weyer, Miss, 11
Veasey, R. G., 16
Veitch & Sons, 114, 116, 117, 118
Venables & Co., 11
Verney, Sir H., 114
Vinnicombe, W., 15
Vinter, H. S., 49

Waggett & Sons, 128
Wales, H.R.H., The Prince of, 58
Walker, J., 9, 84, 93, 95
Warner, W. P., 31
Warrington, Corporation of, 58, 113
Weale, W. H. J., 58, 81, 82, 83, 98
Webb, J., 51
Weber, Rev. G. V., 85
Welch, C., 56
Welchman, C. W., 82
Wellesley, G. E., 20
Westminster, Dean and Chapter of, 74
Willett, H., 67, 104, 111
Williamson, G., 128, 130
Wilmott, Miss E. A., 7, 20, 51, 52, 78
Wilson, A., 104, 106, 131
——, R., 52
Windsor, Trustees of the late H. B., 44.
Withers, E., 36
——, G., 7, 8, 11, 19, 31, 32
Wybard, H. J., 20, 45, 116
Wood, W., 3

Yarborough, Earl of, 6
Yeatman, M., 56
Yeo, H. V., 14, 17
Yorkshire Philosophical Society, 58
Young, W., 116

INDEX OF EXHIBITS.

———◆◇◆———

Note.——Owing to the pressing demand for this Catalogue it has been necessary to issue the First Edition before the completion of the Index of Musical Loans ; a few of the objects frequently asked for are, however, indicated below, and a complete Index to the Exhibits will be published in the Second Edition.

LONDON: PRINTED BY WILLIAM CLOWES AND SONS, LIMITED, STAMFORD STREET AND CHARING CROSS.

CPSIA information can be obtained
at www.ICGtesting.com
Printed in the USA
BVHW042220090221
599727BV00005B/947